RARE BRITISH BREEDS

ENDANGERED SPECIES IN THE UK

For my mother, Charlotte,
Flapjack, Bluebelle and Lady

RARE
BRITISH
BREEDS

ENDANGERED SPECIES IN THE UK

SOPHIE McCALLUM

WHITE OWL

AN IMPRINT OF PEN & SWORD BOOKS LTD.
YORKSHIRE – PHILADELPHIA

First published in Great Britain in 2020 by White Owl
An imprint of
Pen & Sword Books Ltd
Yorkshire - Philadelphia

ISBN 9781526763631

A CIP catalogue record for this book is available from the British Library.

Design: Paul Wilkinson

Printed and bound in India by Replika Press Pvt. Ltd

Pen & Sword Books Ltd incorporates the Imprints of Pen & Sword Books
Archaeology, Atlas, Aviation, Battleground, Discovery, Family History,
History, Maritime, Military, Naval, Politics, Railways, Select, Transport,
True Crime, Fiction, Frontline Books, Leo Cooper, Praetorian Press,
Seaforth Publishing, Wharncliffe and White Owl.

For a complete list of Pen & Sword titles please contact

PEN & SWORD BOOKS LIMITED
47 Church Street, Barnsley, South Yorkshire, S70 2AS, England
E-mail: enquiries@pen-and-sword.co.uk
Website: www.pen-and-sword.co.uk

or

PEN AND SWORD BOOKS
1950 Lawrence Rd, Havertown, PA 19083, USA
E-mail: Uspen-and-sword@casematepublishers.com
Website: www.penandswordbooks.com

CONTENTS

INTRODUCTION

WHEN I WAS YOUNG, I grew up with chickens, and sheep that would disappear every year – only to return, cut up and in small plastic bags, reputedly with their head on top of this arrangement.

As I grew older we moved to a beautiful farmhouse in Hampshire that had a bit of land and I was lucky enough to get a Connemara pony. My mother kept Greyface Dartmoor sheep, Angora goats and an assortment of ducks, chickens and bantams that seemed forever to happily litter the place.

I was first intrigued by the idea of British native breeds when I saw a stand at Countryfile Live in August 2016. Sheep were displayed that would have been around from 5,000 years ago to the present day and the differences were staggering.

It was not until I sent a proposal to publishers for my book *World's Most Endangered* about critically endangered species worldwide that I received an enlightened reply saying: 'But what of our own critically endangered species? Blue Albion cattle – now extinct. Polled Suffolk cattle, Tamworth

Mulgrave Royal Emperor, Cleveland Bay stallion at Castlerise Stud. Brian Comb

pigs, Cleveland Bay horses, Scottish wild cats – all critically endangered.' This struck a chord in me as I used to own a fabulous four-year-old Cleveland Bay cross named Flapjack, and it was because of her that I could not let this go.

Now I find myself writing a book on rare breeds, and all those memories come flooding back to me. I've enjoyed writing about each and every one of these 63 animals and 76 poultry on the Rare Breeds Survival Trust Watchlist, learning about their historical significance and what really makes them unique.

The Rare Breeds Survival Trust is the UK charity working to save British native and rare breeds from extinction. From current registers of breeding females, those most at risk are the Vaynol cattle (12 cows), Cleveland Bay horse (64 mares), Suffolk Horse (80 mares), British Landrace pig (138 sows) and the British Lop pig (161 sows). No endangered breed has become extinct since the RBST was founded in 1973.

I would like to thank the Breed Societies who have so generously supplied photographs for this publication.

***

Les Miles kept the only surviving flock of North Holland Blue chickens for decades in his small back garden in Enfield on the outskirts of London, until he died aged 92 in 1992 having made a real difference to poultry conservation. The species had been pivotal in the UK chicken industry from 1934 to 1960 but was supplanted by American hybrid chickens.

If you have a patch of land, however small, maybe you could cherry-pick your breed from this book and keep the DNA of these historical species alive.

SHEEP

VULNERABLE
(500 TO 900 BREEDING FEMALES)

Boreray
Leicester Longwool
Lincoln Longwool
North Ronaldsay
Welsh Mountain Pedigree
Whitefaced Woodland

AT RISK
(900 TO 1,500)

Border Leicester
Castlemilk Moorit
Cotswold
Derbyshire Gritstone
Devon and Cornwall Longwool
Dorset Horn
Hill Radnor
Manx Loaghtan
Portland
Soay
Teeswater
Wensleydale

MINORITY
(1,500 TO 3,000)

Balwen
Devon Closewool
Dorset Down
Greyface Dartmoor
Llanwenog
Norfolk Horn
Oxford Down

VULNERABLE (500 TO 900)

BORERAY

- To get onto the island of Boreray, conditions have to be calm and one must clamber onto the rocks or jump into the sea.
- In the past, if a St Kilda resident wanted to take some sheep from the island, they would have to throw them into the sea, where an anxious vessel would await them.
- Like other primitive breeds, the Boreray is usually killed as hogget or mutton.
- Both sexes have spiralling horns, the ram's being especially resplendent.
- The Boreray is ideal for conservation grazing – succeeding where other sheep might fail.

Overview

The Boreray is a primitive sheep, hardy enough to be able to survive in a harsh environment. They seem to be generally disease resistant, particularly to foot rot and flystrike. They have a lambing percentage of 140 per cent, and lamb well into their teens. They can shed their own fleece naturally.

The island of Boreray in the St Kilda archipelago.

History

St Kilda is an archipelago, west of the Outer Hebrides. The island of Boreray is found four miles north-east of the remaining islands of St Kilda. It is a difficult island to access, known as 'The Fortress'. Erosion by the waves have created sea stacks. To get onto the island, conditions have to be calm, and one must clamber onto the rocks or jump into the sea. Then there is a steep climb in order to reach the local flora. In the past, if a St Kilda resident wanted to take some sheep from the island, they would have to throw them into the sea, where an anxious vessel would await them.

St Kilda is home to several breeds of sheep. The roots of these go back to the Iron Age, where the sheep inhabited most of northern and western Europe. The Scottish Dunface, also known as the Old Scottish Shortwool, evolved from these Iron Age sheep, sharing many of the same characteristics. They were found throughout the Islands and Highlands of Scotland, up until the late eighteenth century. Breeds, such as the Boreray, the North Ronaldsay and the Shetland all originate from the Dunface. They were further bred with the Scottish Blackface, which became popular in the late nineteenth century, and the pure Scottish Tan Face, which is now extinct. They are the only remaining descendant of the Scottish Tan Face.

In 1930 the islands of St Kilda were evacuated. Sheep were taken from Hirta, the biggest island, to the safety of the mainland, but the sheep on Boreray were too difficult to reach. They were left as a feral herd, where they remain today.

There are Boreray sheep on the mainland. They have all descended (and been registered), from sheep taken from Boreray by the Brathay Expedition in 1971. They were taken by ABRO (Animal Breeds Research Organisation, now known as the Roslin Institute at the University of Edinburgh) to research the Boreray's wool composition and quality.

Appearance

The breed is small. Ewes weigh about 30kg and rams are 45kg. Ewes stand at 55cm at the withers. They tend to have a cream fleece with white legs and face. Typically, there are small patches of black or tan over the body, face and legs. Occasionally a dark sheep will appear. Rams will often have a darker 'collar' around their necks.

Both sexes have spiralling horns, the ram's being especially resplendent. His horns are used in the making of shepherds' crooks. This short-tailed breed has the ability to shed their own fleece naturally. The wool is rough, and it is used for tweeds or carpets yarns.

Conservation Grazing

The Boreray is ideal for conservation grazing – succeeding where other sheep might fail. Its native conditions are so harsh that it is able to go into grazing sites to help improve the biodiversity of the area. However, since numbers are so low – most of the population is feral; this area of expertise has yet to be capitalised on. The breed historically was used for meat and wool.

Meat

Like other primitive breeds, the Boreray is usually killed as a hogget or mutton, hence gaining a larger carcass. The meat is rich in flavour. Due to low numbers, cross-breeding has not occurred with the Borerays.

Wool

The wool has a staple length of 10–15cm and a fleece weighs 1.25kg.

The Boreray Today

Numbers of Boreray sheep have been growing year on year since 2012. In 1999, there were thought to be 74 ewes and a grand total of 84 sheep. By 2002, estimates indicated between 92–100 animals. 2012 saw a huge increase, with 204 ewes registered, and as the years went by to 2017, numbers grew so that the RBST could take the animals out of the Critical category and into the Vulnerable, since it believed the number of breeding ewes to be above 500. The United Nations Food and Agriculture Organisation (FAO) however, listed only 426 breeding ewes in 2017.

Information is taken from the herd books that are collated by breed societies, which are then multiplied to take into account the population of feral sheep that cannot be counted.

LEICESTER LONGWOOL

- The Leicester Longwool was among the first pure bred sheep to have been transported to Australia, reaching those shores in 1826.
- The Breed Society was created in the UK in 1893.
- There have always been black Leicester Longwools but for years they have been sent off to slaughter. In 1986 they were finally accepted for registration.
- Research is being carried out at Cardiff University to see if they can determine a gene denoting fleece colour.
- Other research at York University is analysing parchments, which are made predominantly from sheep skin and contain hair follicles.

Naming

The Leicester Longwool is known by other names, such as Leicester, Bakewell Leicester, Dishley Leicester, Improved Leicester and New Leicester.

Selective Breeding

They were developed at Dishley Grange in Leicester over 200 years ago, in the eighteenth century by the sheep breeding pioneer and agricultural innovator Robert Bakewell (1725–1795). Bakewell was at the forefront of selective breeding and improving agricultural practices. Some of his projects involved the selective breeding of Shire horses and Longhorn cattle, and he spent time on agricultural drainage systems as well as working with turnips and cabbages.

Agricultural Revolution

The Leicester sheep in the 1700s were predominantly found in the Midlands.

They were slow to mature and roughly boned. Bakewell used the Lincoln and Ryeland sheep to work on the Leicester, providing a large framed sheep that produced a sizable amount of wool and meat. This led to increased food production, which in conjunction with other agricultural projects, caused a boom in population and enhanced health. This selective breeding was part of the Agricultural Revolution in Britain in the eighteenth century. Other causes were the removal of common property rights to land and novel methods of cropping, using clover and turnips. The Agricultural Revolution of the eighteenth century created the circumstances needed for the Industrial Revolution in Britain.

Worldwide Populations

Today, partly due to their ability to live in exposed conditions and survive in many different regions, including hilly and mountainous zones, Leicester Longwools are found in Australia, New Zealand, Sweden and the United States. The Leicester Longwool was among the first pure breed sheep to have been transported to Australia, arriving in 1826. The Breed Society was created in the UK in 1893.

Improving other Breeds

They have been widely used to improve other breeds mainly due to their meaty carcass and weighty fleece. Breeds such as the Wensleydale, Lleyn, Border Leicester and Ile de France can all trace their ancestry back to the Leicester Longwool.

Black Leicester Longwools

There have always been black Leicester Longwalls. Bakewell even had one in his flock, but for years they have been sent off to slaughter. But in 1986 they were finally accepted for registration and their own flock book has been established, albeit on a different register to the white sheep.

DNA Research into Fleece Colour

Research is being carried out at Cardiff University to see if they can determine if there is a gene denoting fleece colour. The results of these tests will help breeders concentrate on the strength and diversity of their flock. Other research at York University is analysing parchments, which are made predominantly from sheep skin and contain hair follicles. Using this information, DNA breakdowns can advise researchers on the breed and place of origin of the species. Researchers believe they contain DNA from the 'Improved Leciesters' produced by Bakewell.

Characteristics

The sheep is tall, with long legs and a dense, long, silky fleece. It is hardy, but, like other longwools, it does not do well in prolonged wet conditions. Rams weigh around 100–150kg, whilst ewes are 80–100kg. They do not have any wool on their face and legs and both sexes are polled. They lack the high neck carriage of other longwools and have wide, thickset shoulders which are characteristic of the breed. The sheep is large, sturdy, wide and square with a great body capacity – all key features of the breed.

Cross-breeding

Rams are used commercially to produce heavyweight lambs and hoggets for particular markets. Rams are sometimes used on hill breeds to create halfbred ewes, but Teeswater sheep, among others, are preferred as they have a higher lambing percentage.

Meat

The purebred lamb can weigh 18.9kg at eight weeks old. They are usually slaughtered at 4–5 months with a carcass weight of 20kg. However, chefs are now requiring mutton killed at 18 months for slow cooking for roasts and casseroles.

Wool

The wool should be heavy, long and lustrous with a uniform texture. Growth is 3cm a month and is cream or white, depending on the available nutrients in the soil. Coloured wool has found popularity with spinners. Fleeces fetch a high price – double what some commercial flocks can expect. As a rare breed, the wool is free from the Wool Board directives and can be directly marketed. Staple length is 20–25cm. Fleeces weigh 5–7.5kg with a quality of 40–46s.

LINCOLN LONGWOOL

- Lincoln, as a city, gained a reputation for sheep production in the Middle Ages, when fortunes were to be made from wool. The wool market was fundamental to the economy of the country as a whole, and Lincoln was one of seven officially exporting towns.
- The fleece is extremely heavy. On the sheep it will grow 2.5cm per month.
- Oil-based fibres came onto the market in the 1960s and a decade later the breed was at a critical point.

This breed, otherwise known as the Lincoln, is the biggest sheep in Britain, bred to produce the longest, most substantial and glossiest fleece around. The breed was well sought after and exported all over the world to improve the bulk and calibre of wool in indigenous breeds.

Characteristics

The Lincoln Longwool is a hardy breed, with the added advantage of being notably disease resistant. It is a docile sheep and therefore easy to handle, despite its great size. It has a bare white head and neither sex has horns. Lambing percentages are about 150 per cent and lambs are comparatively small. The fleece of the Lincoln Longwool is extremely luxurious with a long staple length of 20–46cm, yielding 60–80 per cent. It has an exceptional mutton carcass and is suitable for low input, extensive farming.

Wool

The fleece is exceptionally heavy, weighing 8–10kg, and used frequently in hand spinning. On the sheep it will grow 2.5cm per month.

Meat

At eight weeks a pure-bred lamb weighs up to 21.1kg. By five to six months this weight will have increased to a deadweight of 20kg. More often than not,

Stock

Lincoln Longwool Sheep Breeders Association

the lamb is taken on to 9–12 months, as the carcass is lean and will weigh in the region of 30kg.

Beginnings

The Lincoln Longwool was originally a highly sought after breed of sheep in the UK. It produced not only a massive fleece, with hard-wearing, radiant wool, resplendent in lanolin, but it also had the advantage of a huge mutton carcass that provided meat and tallow (an animal fat used to make candles and soap). Lincoln, as a city, had made a name for itself for sheep production during the Middle Ages, when fortunes were to be made in wool. The wool market was fundamental to the economy of the country as a whole, and Lincoln was one of seven officially exporting towns.

1750–1840 Developments

The breed was mentioned in John Mortimer's book, *The Whole Art of Husbandry* in 1707 where he comments, 'Lincolnshire in the Salt Marshes breeds the largest sheep.'

In 1796 the first society concentrating on the breeding of Lincoln Longwools was established. This society was formed on the back of the work done by Robert Bakewell, who used the Old Lincoln to improve his Dishley sheep in Leicester. The work done by this society led the way to the Lincoln Longwool Sheep Breeders' Association that we know today, which was formed in 1892.

1840–1940 Exporting

The Lincolns had great popularity all over the world and were exported widely to improve and evolve additional breeds. South America, New Zealand and Australia saw the most imports. Rams went for extremely high prices: one was sold for 1,450 guineas in 1906.

1950s Popularity Draining

The Second World War saw the fashion in Lincoln Longwools decline. The market in overseas trade of the breed had collapsed due to demand already being fulfilled: Lincoln Longwool genes and sheep had already flooded the market.

Oil-based fibres came onto the market in the 1960s and a decade later the breed was at a critical point. Notably, three breeders, Watts, Read and Bird, saved the sheep from extinction by preserving their bloodlines and continuing to take them to agricultural shows.

1980s–1990s

The Lincoln continued their upward spiral, so that by 1990 there were 100 registered herds. In their heyday of 1900 there had been 350 flocks, so this was quite an achievement. However, commercially, the demand for their wool is still low and the Downs sheep have proved more popular for meat.

News Today

Today most flocks can be found in Lincolnshire. These numbers are in decline from 1990 populations, so the breed does need to be carefully managed.

NORTH RONALDSAY

- The marine iguana, in the Galapagos Islands, is the only other animal known to survive on seaweed.
- The sheep favour brown kelps and have developed a unique metabolism to digest this food.
- They have a high sensitivity to copper and are at risk if put to grass, as the copper in this diet creates toxicity that can be fatal.

Key Characteristics

The North Ronaldsay sheep, also known as the Orkney, are found on the northern most island of Orkney, off the north coast of Scotland. They are a small breed belonging to the northern short-tailed group. DNA evidence shows that they are an extremely close match to Bronze Age sheep found at Skara Brae dating back to 3,000BC.

The North Ronaldsay sheep live entirely on seaweed. This diet has evolved through the building of a huge, dry stone wall around the island, which restrict the sheep solely to the shoreline.

The largest flock is found on North Ronaldsay, but in 1974 the RBST established a second flock on the island of Linga Holm which they purchased for this reason. 150 sheep were sent to the island and a further 28 were bought to the mainland. This was done to protect the sheep from any possible dangers, such as an oil spill in the North Sea.

History

North Ronaldsay sheep date back 5,000 years, possibly being the first ovines to inhabit the UK. Since they have been so isolated they have not been crossed, as many other breeds have, with Roman and European varieties from abroad. They are a member of the Northern Short-Tailed primitive breeds of sheep that also include the Manx Loaghtan, Soay, Shetland and Icelandic sheep.

In 1832, a dry stone wall was erected around the island of North Ronaldsay. It is 19km long, circling the entire island, and stands 1.8m high. Its purpose was to keep the domestic North Ronaldsay sheep away from the sea shore, where seaweed was farmed. This seaweed had a high content of iodine, which was commercially extracted. However, this business became unprofitable and the sheep were exiled to a life on the sea shore, so that more productive cattle could take their place in the fields. The sheep became feral and a genetically isolated breed.

The wall is now an 'A' Listed structure and is one of the longest dry stone walls in existence. Also Listed are nine sheep enclosures called 'punds' or 'pounds', where the sheep are bought in twice yearly for shearing, lambing, counting and slaughtering. Lambing and counting take place between February and May and unusually slaughtering is carried out in winter. This is when the sheep are at their fattest; there being more seaweed available at this time. Shearing takes place in the summer.

1839 saw the creation of the North Ronaldsay sheep court. This body looked after the structure of the wall and the sheep, including ownership. The sheep court is still looking after the sheep to this day, although the European Union would like it to be restructured into a Grazing Committee.

Appearance

As a descendant of the primitive European short-tailed sheep, the Ronaldsay naturally does have a short tail. They have fine bones and are a small sheep. Rams weigh about 30kg and ewes are 25kg or less. They stand 41cm at the withers.

Fleeces come in a range of colours from white to grey, black or brown. Sheep can shed their own fleece, or can be plucked (rooed) instead of shorn. Rams have horns, whilst 20 per cent of ewes are horned; the remainder are polled or scurred (where they have small, poorly formed horns - more common in ewes). They have a small head, and the ewes face is dished i.e. it curves inwards. Ewes are good mothers, giving birth easily, with a lambing percentage of 140 per cent.

Conservation Grazing

The sheep is useful for conservation grazing as it is used to foraging over large distances looking for food. It is also capable of surviving on less food than bigger breeds.

Wool

The North Ronaldsay sheep has two layers in their coat. The undercoat is soft and fine, used for undergarments. The outer coat is coarse with longer hairs that protect the sheep in their harsh environment. These fibres are very durable and tend to be used for over garments.

Even though the sheep is small, it historically was kept for its wool. This wool comes in a spectrum of colours with a fleece weight of about 1kg, a staple length of 10cm and a quality of 53-56s.

Diet

This sheep's diet is made up almost entirely of seaweed. The marine iguana, in the Galapagos Islands, is the only other animal known to survive on seaweed.

Sheep favour brown kelps and have developed a unique metabolism to digest this food. They have a high sensitivity to copper and are at risk if put to grass, as the copper in this diet creates toxicity that can be fatal.

The North Ronaldsay is unique amongst sheep for another reason. Rather than feeding during the day and digesting or ruminating at night as most sheep do, the North Ronaldsay will feed twice daily at low tide, beginning 3.5 hours after high tide, when the kelp is beginning to appear. Rumination of this feed will begin four hours later, after low tide, when the sea is starting to advance once more. This behaviour prevents the sheep becoming stranded by high tide.

Unsurprisingly, the sheep are very salt tolerant. They do have a few freshwater sources in the lakes and ponds around the shore, but they are able to cope much better than other breeds of sheep with breaking down elements present in the salt.

Meat

The sheep are not slaughtered as lambs, as they are too small to be eaten. Instead they are left for hogget or mutton. The meat has a wonderful flavour due to its slow maturation, and 15 months is generally considered the best time to eat them. The meat is lean and has a rich, distinctly gamey taste. It is dark in colour, partially due to the abundant iodine in the sheep's diet.

The European Union states that only pure bred lambs can be sold as 'Orkney Lamb'.

Conservation

The North Ronaldsay Sheep Fellowship maintain the flock book, which was established in 1974. This registers the pure bred animals, and records fewer than 600 breeding females with a total flock size of about 3,700 animals. The sheep are in a highly localised area, which is a risk in itself.

WELSH MOUNTAIN PEDIGREE

- The Welsh Mountain Pedigree dates back from the thirteenth century where it was selectively bred as a hill sheep.
- The Welsh mountains face some of the most demanding climatic conditions in terms of exposure and subsequent food availability.
- A ewe must be able to live and birth on these hills turning poor grade grass into valuable meat products.
- Ewes are amazing mothers, very quick to give birth and endowed with plenty of milk, which is necessary to bring the lambs on quickly so that they can survive and thrive in their environment.
- The ewes require no extra feed, apart from in really appalling weather, and in the lambing season, if the grazing is particularly poor. A lambing percentage of 140–150 per cent can be anticipated.

Thirteenth century Roots

The Welsh Mountain Pedigree dates back from the thirteenth century where it was selectively bred as a hill sheep, particularly in the south of the country. Nowadays the Welsh Mountain Sheep Society (Pedigree Section) concentrates on improving the gene pool as well as showing the sheep. They have been recognised at national shows, winning the supreme class several times.

Many Sheep

Many different types of sheep graze the Welsh Mountains, but the pedigree sheep are of medium build with a wide forehead and muzzle. They have a white to tanned face and legs, with a black or freckled nose and white fleece. Only the rams have horns.

Demanding Climatic Conditions

The Welsh mountains face some of the most demanding climatic conditions in terms of exposure and subsequent food availability; and the ability to thrive on these hills makes the sheep renowned for their hardiness. There is a wide-ranging difference in the landscape and weather patterns in Wales so it is unsurprising that there will also be differences in the sheep.

Converting Poor Grade Grass into Valuable Meat

A ewe must be able to live and birth on these hills turning poor grade grass into valuable meat products. Whilst she is able to complete this task she also has the ability to gain 50 per cent of her own weight if taken to lowland pastures.

Success on the British Markets

Rams are renowned for their breeding; used to enhance size, conformation and wool quality. They are used to cross-breed with both lowland and hill ewes, improving the quality of lamb meat, which is highly regarded for its succulence, leanness, and wonderful flavour, so much so that it is very successful on the British market. Welsh Mountain Pedigree lamb, from the hills, can be bought from July to December each year.

Milk to Survive and Thrive

Ewes are amazing mothers, very quick to give birth and endowed with plenty of milk, which is necessary to bring the lambs on quickly so that they can survive and thrive in their environment. The ewes require no extra feed, apart from in really appalling weather, and in the lambing season, if the grazing is particularly poor. A lambing percentage of 140–150 per cent can be anticipated. Fleeces are heavier than those of lowland breeds, as you would expect.

WHITEFACED WOODLAND

- The Whitefaced Woodland is one of the largest native hill breeds.
- It is often crossed with different hill breeds to increase their size and strength, without forfeiting hardiness.
- Ewes can keep producing lambs well into their teens, which is very fertile for a hill breed.
- The fleece takes up dyes very well and is mainly used in carpets.

Origins

The Whitefaced Woodland sheep originally came from the South Pennines, on the borders of Yorkshire and Derbyshire. It is also known as the Penistone sheep, named after the Yorkshire town where sheep sales have been carried out since 1699. It is thought to have origins with the Swaledale and Lonk sheep. Other influences in its evolution are the Cheviot and Merino. The Merino sheep was inaugurated into the breed by the Duke of Devonshire in the beginning of the nineteenth century.

Appearance

The Whitefaced Woodland is one of the largest native hill breeds. A ram can weigh as much as 130kg. Mature ewes average 60kg on the scales, but can amount to 72.5kg when kept on the quality grazing of lowland fields. They are however, suited and used to sparse grazing and rocky topography and their strong and hardy physique reflects that. Both ewes and rams have heavy horns that spiral around their face. In keeping with their name, they have white faces, heads and legs. Their tail is long if left undocked.

Cross-breeding

The Whitefaced Woodland ram is often crossed with different hill breeds to increase their size and strength, without forfeiting hardiness. The Whitefaced Woodland ewe is a low input ewe that can be used in lowland farms, producing good offspring when crossed with a terminal ram, producing lambs for slaughter rather than breeding.

Lambing

Ewes are strong, large and very milky with superb maternal instincts. Lambing tends to be uncomplicated, with lambs being sturdy and energetic. Ewes can keep producing lambs well into their teens, which is very fertile for a hill breed. When put to a terminal sire, resulting lambs are of exceptional quality and bred at a low cost. A lambing percentage of 150 per cent is reached on the hills, and this can increase to 200 per cent down on the lowland.

Meat

The Whitefaced Woodland is known as a meat breed, unlike many of its hill sheep friends. A pure bred lamb reaches a deadweight of 18–20kg in five months with a good grade on it. The meat is lean, so the lambs can be killed at 1–2 years, (hogget age), which gives the meat a deeper red colour compared to a younger lamb, with greater flavour.

Peter Mawson

Wool

The first sheering of a ewe is said to beget the greatest quality of fleece. The addition of Merino sheep into the breed certainly increased the quality of the wool, especially when compared to other hill sheep. The wool has a quality of 44-50s, with a staple length of around 15cm (which is the average length of wool). Fleeces weigh in the region of 2–3kg. It can be used today for knitting and hand-spinning, blending it with mohair or silk for added effect. It takes up dyes very well and is mainly used in carpets.

Conservation Grazing

The Whitefaced Woodland sheep is a good conservation grazer in that it can cope with meagre situations and will eat otherwise unprofitable plants and shrubs.

Present Day

There are sizable, commercial flocks of the Whitefaced Woodland, kept in the South Pennines, where they first came from.

BORDER LEICESTER

- The Border Leicester has its roots in the Dishley Leicester bred by the agricultural pioneer, Robert Bakewell (1726–1795) in Dishley, Leicester.
- Bakewell quickly realised that running all sheep together, as they were at the time, with random breeding, creating a plethora of different breeds with their own arbitrary characteristics, was not constructive.
- Through meticulous selection he created the new breed: the New Leicester, or Dishley Leicester, as it became known.
- Two brothers, George and Matthew Culley, had been apprentices of Bakewell in 1763. They settled in Northumberland and took with them a herd of Bakewell's new sheep.
- The brothers held a yearly sale of both ewes and rams and provided a service leasing rams.
- This led to two unmistakable types of Dishley Leicester evolving: one in Northumberland and the other in the Scottish Borders. The hardier type were favoured by the Border farmers and by around 1850 this variant began to be called the Border Leicester.
- The breed was exported widely, and in Australia, which they reached in 1871, they are today used to produce a large percentage of meat sales.
- They are historically known as 'The Great Improver' due to their capacity for improving the offspring of any sheep that they are bred with.

Pioneers in an Agricultural Revolution

The Border Leicester has its roots in the Dishley Leicester bred by Robert Bakewell (1726–1795) in Dishley, Leicester. Bakewell was an agricultural pioneer, especially in the field of selective breeding of sheep, cattle and horses. His work followed on from other leading figures in the farming world: Jethro Tull, who invented the seed drill, and Lord 'Turnip' Townshend, who developed the system of four field crop rotation. Both Tull and Townshend were major influences on England's 'Agricultural Revolution' which took place between 1750 and 1800, and which achieved massively improved farm technology and productivity, needed to support a huge increase in the UK population at this time and in the years to come.

Mating Free-for-All

Bakewell quickly realised that running all sheep together, as they were at the time, with random breeding, creating a plethora of different breeds with their own arbitrary characteristics, was not constructive. He organised a structure of 'in-and-in' breeding whereby he only allowed breeding between animals that bore a close relationship, in what is nowadays known as line breeding. Popular thinking is that he chose the old Lincolnshire sheep and mated them with the local Leicestershire sheep, and with meticulous selection and culling he was able to attain the sought-after qualities of excellent meat and lambing potential. He called this new breed the 'New Leicester' but it quickly became known as the 'Dishley Leicester'.

Eleanor S

1,200 Guinea Mating Charge

These new sheep proved marketable. Bakewell began to hire out the rams to nearby counties. In 1760 he charged 17 shillings 6d per ram. This rose to 1,000 guineas for 20 rams in 1786 and by 1789, he accumulated 1,200 guineas for only three rams – a vast sum of money.

Two Brothers Go It Alone

Two brothers, George and Matthew Culley, had been apprentices of Bakewell in 1763. They lived and worked throughout Northumberland before putting down roots in the Glendale region of that county in 1767. They bought with them a number of Dishley Leicesters. As time wore on, these sheep began to find new owners on both sides of the Scottish border, as the brothers held a yearly sale of both ewes and rams. The brothers also provided a service leasing rams for 50–200 guineas for the breeding period.

Bluecaps and Redlegs

This led to two unmistakable types of Dishley Leicesters evolving: one in Northumberland and the other in the Scottish Borders. In Northumberland, the brothers had begun crossing them with Teeswater sheep, whilst in the Borders the cross was with Cheviot sheep. The two different types were called the 'Bluecaps' and the 'Redlegs'. The hardier redlegs were favoured by the Border farmers and by around 1850 this variant began to be called the Border Leicester. The dark faced bluecaps were called the Bluefaced Leicester, as they are today.

Extensive Export

The breed rapidly gained popularity and were widespread in the UK by the nineteenth century. They were exported globally, and registered flocks can be found in British Guiana, Canada, China, Colombia, South Africa, France, Spain, Portugal, United States, India, Japan, Yugoslavia, Iran, Hungary, Russia, Turkey and Switzerland. In Australia, which they reached in 1871, they are today used to produce a large percentage of meat sales, by breeding first with a Merino ewe, whose lambs provide a first-class meat product. From this cross, the subsequent ewes are bred with a shortwool ram, such as Poll Dorset or Southdown. Progeny will grow quickly to commercial weights and their carcase configuration is said to be perfect.

Widespread Breeding Stock

Also in Australia, the Gromark sheep, which have been selected for good growth rates since 1965, have a 50 per cent Border Leicester and 50 per cent Corriedale make up.

New Zealand received the breed in 1859, where it has been used to originate the Border–Romney cross (Coopworth) and the Border–Corriedale (Borderdale) stock.

In the US, the first breed association was created in 1888. At present two associations exist – the American Border Leicester Association and the North American Border Leicester Association.

Closer to Home

The Border Leicester has historically been known as 'The Great Improver'. It owes this title to its great capacity for improving the offspring of any sheep that it is bred with: whether that lamb is a ewe to be used for breeding, or a wether lamb (a male sheep castrated before sexual maturity) fit for our demanding meat market. Breeders highly value the Border Leicester genetics and use the ram on hill ewes: for example, the North Country Cheviot, to create the Scotch Halfbred; the Welsh Mountain, to create the Welsh Halfbred; and the Blackface ewe, giving the Greyface. Other breeds, such as the Suffolk, Texel crosses and Lleyn ewes also benefit from Border Leicester blood.

Striking Roman Nose

The breed has won umpteen prizes in carcass and liveweight classes. A ram, measured for its liveweight will lie in the region of 120–145kg, whilst a ewe will be 80–100kg. They are white sheep with a long body and wide, sturdy back. They have a large Roman nose and they possess large, upright ears. Their impressive, graceful appearance makes them admired in the show ring. They are very calm and ewes make good mothers, with a lambing percentage of 165–180 per cent. Rams can be crossed with even the smallest of ewes, such as the Welsh Mountain. Fleeces weigh in the region of 6–9kg for a ram, and 4–6kg for a ewe, with a quality of 48-50s.

Bradford Count and Micron Grade

The Bradford Count is derived from the city of Bradford, before microscopes and lasers were invented. Knowledgeable workers would judge how many 560-yard hanks of individual yarn would be spun by a skilled spinner from a pound of 'top'. A top is the cleaned and combed wool, lying with all strands aligned. The thinner the wool diameter, the greater the number of hanks that could be spun. The numerical figure denotes the number of hanks that could be spun. For example, a fine wool might give 80 hanks, whereas a stronger wool, maybe only 36s. Fibre diameter can now also be measured by microns. A micron or micrometre is one millionth of a metre. Border Leicester sheep have a micron grade of 29–32. This is opposite to the Bradford count, in that fine fibres have a lower value. Each fleece has a range of factors, such as health and age of the sheep, and nutrition, which all have a bearing on fibre diameters.

CASTLEMILK MOORIT

- This breed was developed by Sir Jock Buchanan-Jardine on his Castlemilk Estate in Dumfriesshire.
- The Castlemilk Moorit is one of the bigger primitive types of lowland sheep. They are a graceful breed, being long-legged and agile.
- The word 'Moorit' is derived from a Lowland Scots word which indicates the pale tan or reddish-brown colouration of their fleeces.
- The Castlemilk Moorit fleece is typically moulted or rooed – which means plucked – instead of being shorn.
- Sheep mature slowly but surely, giving a delicious, fine grained, lean meat.

Selectively Breed for a Kemp Free Fleece

This breed was developed by Sir Jock Buchanan-Jardine on his Castlemilk Estate in Dumfriesshire. He wanted to create a breed of sheep that would

adorn his parkland and supply fine, kemp-free moorit coloured wool to garb his staff. He used Manx Loghtan sheep, moorit Shetland and the wild Mouflon in his breeding programme. Sir John died in 1970, and most of his flock was culled. A few were dispersed. John Henson saved six ewes and a ram, which he took to Cotswold Farm Park. All Castlemilk Moorits alive today owe their existence these few sheep.

Graceful, Long-Legged and Agile

The Castlemilk Moorit is one of the bigger primitive types of lowland sheep with rams weighing in at 55kg and ewes at 40kg. They are a graceful breed, being long-legged and agile. They have a clean head with ewes sporting two matching widespread horns. The rams' horns are even bigger, with uniform spirals that steer clear of the cheeks. The sheep will often show their ancestry, with white mouflon markings, on the 'spectacles', belly, lower jaw, leg patches and buttocks. The word 'Moorit' is derived from a Lowland Scots word which indicates the pale tan or reddish-brown colouration of their fleeces. The Castlemilk Moorit fleece is typically moulted or rooed – which means plucked – instead of being shorn. This fleece contains hardly any, if any, kemp and is sought after by hand spinners. The Staple length is 4–7cm; fleeces tend to weigh 1kg; and the grade is 48s to 50s.

Taking their Time to get to the Table

The breed is generally hardy but may need some protection during lambing. They seem to be impervious to flystrike and footrot. Ewes are wonderful mothers, lambing throughout their long life and generating little, energetic lambs. They have a lambing percentage of 160–170 per cent if well looked after. Sheep mature slowly but surely, giving a delicious, fine grained, lean meat.

COTSWOLD

- Archaeological evidence indicates that their ancestors were introduced by the Romans.
- Cirencester was a major centre for the sheep trade in 100AD continuing right through to the thirteenth century where it was reported that huge flocks were raised on the hills.
- Throughout the reign of Edward III, in the fourteenth century, 30,000 sacks of wool were given to the King's household each year.
- By the fifteenth century, Cotswold sheep and wool were highly valued exports, so much so that in 1425, King Henry VI decreed that 'no sheep shall be exported without the King's licence' and records of the time show that only Cotswolds sheep were allowed to be exported.
- The first Cotswold arrived in New York State in 1832 and by 1914 there were more than 75,000 Cotswold sheep in the US and Canada, as recorded by the American Cotswold Record Association.
- After the First World War, numbers had fallen dramatically due to the disappearing wool trade. By the middle of the twentieth century only one breeding flock in the UK remained, with a cluster of smaller flocks.

As Old as the Hills

Archaeological evidence indicates that their ancestors were introduced by the Romans, but from which part of the Roman Empire they originated from is unclear. They are considered to be one of the earliest documented breeds in the UK, even lending their title to the land that they occupied. 'Cotes' refers to a shelter for mammals or birds, and 'Wold' is a piece of open, unproductive land. They really can claim to be as 'Old as the Hills'.

The 'Golden Fleece'

Cirencester was a major centre for the sheep trade in 100AD continuing right through to the thirteenth century where it was reported that huge flocks were raised on the hills. Throughout the reign of Edward III, in the fourteenth century, 30,000 sacks of wool were given to the King's household per year. The Florentines came to England to take back with them wool and

cloth from the Cotswold sheep, which had a reputation for being slightly golden coloured, and became known as the 'Golden Fleece'. The wool was used instead of linen, weaving in fine gold thread to make outfits for kings and priests. By the fifteenth century, Cotswold sheep and wool were highly valued exports, so much so that in 1425, King Henry VI decreed that 'no sheep shall be exported without the King's licence', and records of the time show that only Cotswolds sheep were allowed to be exported. Indeed, in 1437, the King of Portugal chose Cotswold wool over the silkiest of Spanish wool, applying to Henry VI for the pleasure of importing 60 sacks to make up some gold woven garments and finery.

Errant Leicester Genes

The Cotswold sheep of the time were probably a long-legged, large animal with lengthy, substantial wool, now thought to be the biggest and hardiest of all English breeds. Some breeders tried crossing it with the Leicester breed which had been improved by Robert Bakewell; other breeders preferred to keep the breed pure. Whilst the crossing with Leicester sheep was noted to improve the breed in shape and disposition, and to fatten it, it had the tendency to diminish the great hardiness of constitution and reduce the weight of the wool, causing many breeders to return to using pure Cotswold rams to correct the situation. The use of the Leicester also led to colour being introduced into some flocks; many of these sheep were exported to the US, where the Black Cotswold is a recognised breed. Cotswold sheep in the UK must be white and can only be registered with the Cotswold Sheep Society if that is the case. Kemp, or coarse hair, is not usually found in the wool.

The ongoing agricultural revolution led to the emergence of agricultural shows, for example the Royal Show starting in 1839, which, as well as the annual sales of the Cotswold ram, led to the spreading of the sheep across the country.

Popular Improver

The Cotswold has been used to create other breeds, such as the Oxford Down sheep, which is a combination of the Cotswold ram with a Hampshire Down ewe. It has also been used to generate breeds such as the Oldenburgh and Colbred. The Cotswold is a popular improver as it increases the size of the progeny as well as wool yield and the capability to mature on forage. The Cotswold has also been used on the Cheviot, Welsh Mountain, North Country Mule and Suffolk to give good results.

Huge Exports

During the nineteenth century the breed was enjoying enormous success, with demand from America, Australia and the whole of Europe, including a good trade in the UK. 1914 saw more than 75,000 Cotswold sheep in the US and Canada recorded by the American Cotswold Record Association. This was due to the fact that it was preferred to other longwools, as it did not need so much grain to create the desired growth. Additionally, the breed could increase staple length when crossed with other breeds, but at the same time, not losing carcass size or adding to the thickness of the wool.

Long Forelock

Cotswold sheep are good, milky mothers with an excellent maternal instinct. Lambing percentages are 150–175 per cent, and a ten-year-old ewe can easily produce twin lambs. Ewes weigh in the region of 85–90kg, whilst rams are 130kg. They are dual purpose animals with their meat being renowned for its mild flavour and are also excellent mutton producers. They have a staple length of 15–20cm, a fleece weight of 5.5–10kg and a quality of 44s–48s. Both male and female are polled and possess a long forelock, and it was said that when being shorn a patch was left unshorn on the shoulder so that the quality of wool could be seen.

Looking to the Future

After the First World War, numbers had fallen dramatically due to the disappearing wool trade. By the middle of the twentieth century only one breeding flock remained in the UK, with a cluster of smaller flocks. Numbers are growing with the help of a buoyant Cotswold Sheep Society.

DERBYSHIRE GRITSTONE

- The Derbyshire Gritstone is among the oldest native breeds in the UK.
- They were first found in the 1770s, on the hills of the Dale of Goyt (now known as the Goyt Valley), which borders the Peak District, and were originally called the Dale O'Goyt sheep.
- The Derbyshire Gritstone is renowned for its ability to improve other breeds. It increases the body, size and strength of a flock. It has a superior fleece. With both sexes being polled, it will decrease the likelihood of horns in offspring.
- Polled sheep have less problems with headfly damage
- The other plus side to polled sheep came in the form of EU slaughter regulations which governed head-skinning requirements.
- It has a lambing percentage of 145 per cent on low-grade hill ground. It gives the best returns of all hill sheep.
- The breed has recently won champion fleece at the Great Yorkshire Show twice in seven years – the largest show of its kind in the UK.

One of the Oldest Native Breeds

The Derbyshire Gritstone is among the oldest native breeds in the UK. They were first found in the 1770s, on the hills of the Dale of Goyt (now known as the Goyt Valley), which borders the Peak District, and were originally called the Dale O'Goyt sheep. By 1850, farmers were at work improving the breed to get hardy, disease-resistant creatures that would do well on poor grazing and be productive with lambs, meat and wool. Through methodical selection and

careful breeding, awareness of the sheep grew, so that on 15 October 1906, 27 farmers gathered to create the Derbyshire Gritstone Sheepbreeders Society (DGSS) with the 8th Duke of Devonshire as President. The Stud book was inaugurated soon afterwards, with 20 flocks being listed. From these original flocks, Derbyshire Gritstones were soon to be found in Lancashire, Yorkshire, Cheshire, Wales and Scotland (including the Outer Islands).

Best Returns of All Hill Sheep

The Derbyshire Gritstone is renowned for its ability to improve other breeds. It increases the body, size and strength of a flock, causing lambs to finish early with good financial rewards. With both sexes being polled, it will decrease the likelihood of horns in offspring. Its superior fleece enhances the calibre of the wool, and it will improve face and leg markings and colouration in lambs. It has a lambing percentage of 145 per cent on low-grade hill ground. It gives the best returns of all hill sheep.

Polling and the EU

Polling became important in the 1980s. Polled sheep had less problems with headfly damage. This proved vital, as the effects of headfly damage were felt in the lambs' growth, as mothers would become quick-tempered and reluctant to suckle. Sale prices for these lambs would be less, as they had put on a reduced weight. The other plus side to polled sheep came in the form of EU slaughter regulations which governed head-skinning requirements. Polled sheep were faster to deal with and therefore cheaper to put through the abattoir.

Meat and the Market

The Derbyshire Gritstone gives rise to a clean, lean meat carcass which is desired by the market, in addition to high class, top quality mutton. Lambs develop swiftly with rapid maturation engendering a worthy carcass measurement. Hill lambs are fit for slaughter from 68 to 104 days (10 to 15 weeks) with a liveweight of 40kg and a deadweight of 21kg. Male lambs, castrated before reaching sexual maturity – defined as wether lambs – can be kept for market at Christmas.

Championship Fleece

The wool board loves the Derbyshire Gritstone fleece as it is so unblemished and contains no kemp or dark hairs. It is fine and dense, with a staple length of 8–10cm. Fibres can become coarser progressing down the flanks, but some sheep maintain their quality throughout. The quality is 52-56s and a fleece will weigh between 2–3kg. The average yield, which is the percentage of wool remaining after the greasy wool has been removed, is 68 per cent. The wool from the majority of hill sheep is used in the manufacture of carpets, but the Derbyshire Gritstone has such a fine fleece that it can be utilised in the production of hosiery, Worsted yarns and knitwear. The breed has recently won champion fleece at the Great Yorkshire Show twice in seven years – the largest show of its kind in the UK.

Protecting the Insect and Mammal Population

The Derbyshire Gritstone, coming from the desolate hills of the North Country and Wales can amplify agricultural output in those areas, but is also useful for conservation grazing where damage to the insect and small mammal inhabitants is greatly reduced compared to mechanical intervention. Ewes are 55–65kg, rams are 80–100kg. The sheep has a long body with broad, strong shoulders and a well-proportioned frame with good outlines. Its face and legs are clear of wool and the face is black and white. Legs are both black and white, with the front legs having black knee patches. Hooves are also black.

DEVON AND CORNWALL LONGWOOL

- A cross with a terminal ram will produce a lambing percentage of nearly 200 per cent, whilst still preserving the quality of wool and placid nature of the sheep.
- If crossed with a Dorset Horn, ewes are produced that will lamb all year round.
- It is famed for its huge fleeces. They are thought to have the largest fleece of all British breeds.
- Due to the vast quantities of wool, even the lambs are shorn, producing a wool that is highly sought after.

History

The South Devon sheep was a bigger breed, established in South Devon, East and South Cornwall, whilst the smaller Devon Longwool was found in North Cornwall, North Devon and South Somerset. In the early 1900s there was a distinct difference in size between the breeds. The breeds became more similar over the years, so much so that the Flock Book Association of the Devon and Cornwall Longwool was formed on 1 January 1977. This was a merger of the South Devon Flock Book Association and the Devon Longwool Sheep Breeder's Society.

Breeding

The breed is placid and can be bucket trained. They cope with most weather conditions and enjoy grass and fodder crops. These sheep do not need complex fencing. Ewes have few lambing problems and are wonderful mothers, with a lambing percentage of 150 per cent. The breed is kept by small holders and in farming systems for both their meat and their wool.

Cross-breeding

If crossed with a British Milk Sheep, among others, lambs are thought to live much longer. A cross with a terminal ram will produce a lambing percentage of nearly 200 per cent, whilst still preserving the quality of wool and placid nature. If crossed with a Dorset Horn, ewes are produced that will lamb all year round. If crossed with a Bluefaced Leicester, lambing percentages are increased and lambs will gain weight easily and be ready for market early.

Meat

The Devon and Cornwall Longwool sheep have a good food conversion rate. A purebred lamb is ready for slaughter at four months. A weight of 20.5kg is reached by eight weeks. At this stage the lamb is lean and can be left to gain weight before killing. A cross-bred lamb will finish quickly at a good weight.

Wool

The Devon and Cornwall Longwool is famed for its huge fleeces. They are thought to have the largest fleece of all British breeds. Whilst not the finest quality, it is tough and durable and widely used in carpets, rugs and even for doll's hair. Due to the vast quantities of wool, even the lambs are shorn, producing a wool that is highly sought after. An ewe's wool weighs approximately 7–8kg, whilst a ram will produce more than 15kg. The staple length is 20–25cm. The quality is 32s–36s.

Devon and Cornwall Longwool Flockbook Association

Characteristics

The Devon and Cornwall Longwall is a large, well-built sheep with ewes weighing 75–80kg and rams 100–110kg. This breed may be smaller than other longwool breeds but it is more heavily built. Both sexes are polled.

The head is adorned with curly wool, with a white face and black outside lips. The interior lips and tongue are pink. The ears have silky white hair with black spots on the exterior and are pink and hairless on in the interior. The sheep has black hooves and a fleece of long, thick, curly wool with a wide staple.

DORSET HORN

- The most striking feature of this breed is its ability to lamb all year round. Depending on management, it is capable of producing as many as 4–5 lambs per year.
- The native, horned sheep of Dorset were in for a surprise in the sixteenth century, when Spanish ships either sold or smuggled in their valuable Merino sheep. This Spanish breed were able to procreate throughout the year, and subsequently the Dorset Horn emerged.
- The breed became immensely consequential all over the world, and was extensively exported to Australia, North America and South Africa. By the turn of the nineteenth century it was among the most prevalent sheep in the US.
- Success had an edge to it however – the sheep had horns. Polled (hornless) sheep were developed in the US and soon became more popular than the original Dorset Horn.

Can Produce 4–5 Lambs a Year

The most striking feature to this breed is its ability to lamb all year round. Depending on management, which defines the right food and nutrition, it is capable of producing as many as 4–5 lambs per year, with a lambing percentage of 140–200 per cent.

Surprise Spanish Imports

The native, tan-faced, horned sheep of Dorset were in for a surprise in the sixteenth century, when Spanish ships either sold or smuggled in their valuable Merino sheep. This Spanish breed, akin to Portland sheep, were able to procreate throughout the year, and subsequently the Dorset Horn emerged.

They became a familiar sight in the south of the UK, in counties such as Dorset, Somerset and Devon as well as Wales.

Most Prevalent Sheep in the US

History states that it was Richard Scott of Oregon who took the first Dorset Horns to the US in 1860. Subsequent imports were exhibited in Chicago in 1885 and the market for them boomed. In the UK, the initial Flock Book was published in 1892. The breed became immensely consequential all over the world, and was extensively exported to Australia, North America and South Africa. By the turn of the nineteenth century it was among the most prevalent sheep in the US.

Graham C

Edge to Success

Success had an edge to it however – the sheep had horns. North Carolina State University produced the first polled (hornless) ewes in 1949, followed by the first polled ram in 1954. Two years later, in 1956, the polled sheep achieved registration from the Continental Dorset Club which had first registered the Dorset Horn. These sheep, named the Poll Dorset, were imported into the UK, where they achieved massive popularity and soon outnumbered the original Dorset Horn.

Crossings and Terminations

A terminal sire, crossed with a Dorset Horn ewe, creates a quick maturing lamb throughout the year. A Dorset Horn ram is useful to sire ewes that will lamb all year round, with the associated good mothering qualities, milkiness and fast maturation. A purebred lamb can be slaughtered at 10 weeks providing a carcass from 16kg to more than 20kg. Ewes can go on lambing up to the age of 10–12 years. With this productivity it is easy to develop a closed flock, thereby eliminating the threat of disease from imported sheep.

Fleece Quality

Shearing takes place once a year and offers a fleece of between 2.3–4.1kg, yielding 50–70 per cent. The wool is white, very strong and close, with no dark strands. Staple length is 6–10cm with a quality of 54s–58s.

Market for Buttons

The breed thrives worldwide and is docile and easy to manage – coming to the bucket. They are stocky, with ewes weighing 75–85kg and rams 120kg. Their white face has a characteristic pink nose. They are a medium sized sheep with ample body length and good muscle conformation. Both rams and ewes have horn. In the case of the ram, these are heavy and masculine, curling downwards in a spiral, whilst on the ewe they are more elegant and forward curving. The ram will achieve its mature sized horns when it is two years old. These horns can create another market, in that they are hunted down by artisans to carve buttons or handles for walking sticks.

HILL RADNOR

- The Hill Radnor are located on the Radnor Hills on the English and Welsh borders, stretching from Radnor to Hereford, Monmouth to Brecon.
- They are thought to be akin to the old Welsh breed of tan-faced sheep that have been on these hills for centuries.
- They were particularly devastated by the Foot and Mouth cull in 2001, as their area of the UK was hard hit.
- The sheep have found uses in cross-breeding. The Hill Radnor is preferred to the Welsh Mountain as it has the advantages of being bigger, with greater productivity and fertility, and easier to manage.
- A hill flock will have a lambing percentage of 120 per cent, whilst this will increase to 165 per cent with good supervision in the lowlands.

Ancient Hill Sheep

The Hill Radnor are located on the Radnor Hills on the English and Welsh borders, stretching from Radnor to Hereford, and Monmouth to Brecon. They are thought to be akin to the old Welsh breed of tan-faced sheep that have been on these hills for centuries. The first record of the Hill Radnor goes back

Mrs Tracey Ev

to 1911, with the breed society forming in 1949. Populations of these animals are located mainly in the above areas, and they have not spread far throughout the remainder of the UK. They were particularly devastated by the Foot and Mouth cull in 2001, as their area of the UK was hard hit.

Cross-breeding to create a Bigger Lamb with Innate Hardiness

The Hill Radnor has found uses in cross-breeding. Older ewes, also known as draft ewes, are dispatched from their life in the hills and taken to lowland farms where they will be utilised for breeding for a few years. This is a common practice for the Welsh Mountain sheep too, although the Hill Radnor is the preferred option as it has the advantages of being bigger, with greater productivity and fertility, and easier to manage. The Hill Radnor ram is successfully crossed with other hill breeds to create a bigger lamb with superior conformation, whilst still retaining its innate hardiness.

Meatier than the Welsh Mountain

Meat is another market in which the Hill Radnor can find success. They are bigger and more substantial than the Welsh Mountain sheep. A lamb will reach 17kg at eight weeks old and is fit for slaughter at 4–5 months. Often a terminal sire is used to breed with a Hill Radnor ewe creating a rapidly growing, well-formed lamb. Ewes weigh in the region of 50–55kg, whilst rams are 70–80kg. Lambing percentage will vary according to location. A hill flock will have a percentage of 120 per cent, whilst this will increase to 165 per cent with good supervision in the lowlands. Lambs are known to be small and active and the ewes experience few lambing problems. They have excellent maternal qualities.

At Home in the Smallholding

The Hill Radnor fleece is dense and white. Its weight will be 2–2.5kg, Staple length 8–10cm and quality 48–56s.

As a hill breed, these sheep are hardy and are effective on restricted forage. The Hill Radnor has a characteristic tan face with a curved nose. Ewes are polled, whilst rams have horns. They are easy to manage, with a docile nature, and are at home as much in the smallholding as on the hill.

Manx Loaghtan

- The Manx Loaghtan is one of several sheep belonging to the group of Northern short-tailed primitive breeds including the ancient sheep in Scotland, the Hebrides and Shetland Islands, such as the Soay and Shetland.
- It can survive in hill areas where modern sheep would not thrive and has been found in the upland areas of the Isle of Man for centuries.
- In the 1950s, there were only 43 individual sheep left, usurped by more commercial breeds.
- Manx Loaghtan meat is considered a delicacy, with rich, distinctive tastes.
- Research on Ramsey Island, Bardsey Island and the Isle of Man have shown that as numbers of the sheep increase, so does the incidence of breeding cloughs, and when the numbers of sheep decrease, there is a corresponding decrease in the populations of cloughs.
- Most of the time, sheep have four horns, sometimes presenting with two or six. These multi-horned sheep are the result of a splitting gene and it has been shown that when breeding from two-horned sheep no four-horned animals result.
- Rams can get very confrontational during the breeding season. They use their horns to establish dominance. Whilst brain injury is infrequent, broken necks can happen. More usually, injury is caused to the head, neck and horns.
- Occasionally paler rings around the eye, known as 'spectacles' will occur, and it is thought that this is a throwback to cross-breeding with a Castlemilk Morrit ram in 1936 and a Soay ram in 1966 when Manx Loaghtan stocks were low.

The Manx Loaghtan is one of several sheep belonging to the group of Northern short-tailed primitive breeds including the ancient sheep in Scotland, the Hebrides and Shetland Islands, such as the Soay and Shetland. It can survive in hill areas where modern sheep would not thrive and has been found in the upland areas of the Isle of Man for centuries. To begin with, the sheep came in many colourways, including white, grey and black, but it was the brown 'moorit' colour which was desired by weavers and so sheep were selectively bred to attain this colour. Indeed, the sheep is named for the colour 'mouse-brown' which translates in Manx as 'lugh dhoan' or 'Loaghtan'.

Only 43 Sheep Left

In the 1950s, there were only 43 individual sheep left, usurped by more commercial breeds. Manx National Heritage acted and created two flocks

Scott

which are thriving, and subsequently profit-orientated flocks have been set up on the island and the UK mainland, although they are still considered rare.

Meat Considered a Delicacy

Manx Loaghtan meat is thought of as a delicacy, with rich, distinctive tastes. It is often sold as hogget (yearling) or mutton (fully grown) meat to allow the flavour to mature. A 15-month-old sheep will give an 18kg carcass of low fat meat. Most flocks of Manx are unmixed, but terminal sires can be used on a Manx ewe to create a bigger progeny. Manx rams are sometimes used commercially to corroborate uncomplicated birthing as genetically the sheep experience few lambing complications.

More Sheep means More Cloughs

The sheep is also recognised as a conservation grazer. The National Trust for Jersey has introduced Manx Loaghtans on the coastal hills, where their flock has grown considerably from 20 to 231. Research on Ramsey Island, Bardsey Island and the Isle of Man have shown that as numbers of the sheep increase, so does the incidence of breeding cloughs, and when the numbers of sheep decrease, there is a corresponding decrease in the populations of cloughs. It is thought that as the sheep graze and flatten the grassland, they give the birds the opportunity to feed on the surface and soil insects. Their dung also attracts beetles and fly larvae, which the birds feed on.

High Lanolin Content

Manx Loaghtan sheep produce an unusually resilient fleece, and its rich brown hues make it sought after by weavers and spinners. It is used undyed to make woollen and tweeds and contains a high volume of lanolin wax. This is an aid in shearing on sunny days, as the lanolin becomes more fluid. The wool has a staple length of 8–13cm, fleece weight of 1.5kg and a quality of 44s–48s.

Multi-Horned

The Manx Loaghtan are known for their horns, both in the male and female, although they can occasionally be polled. Most of the time, sheep have four horns, sometimes presenting with two or six. These multi-horned sheep are the result of a splitting gene and it has been shown that when breeding from two-horned sheep, no four-horned animals result. The horns should not grow into the face or get in the way of grazing.

Aggression at Breeding Season

Rams can get very confrontational during the breeding season. They use their horns to establish dominance. It is best to pen the rams tightly to avoid too much jostling, charging and backing off. A male lamb is sometimes used for mating as they are less aggressive. Otherwise, rams will present horns to one another, raising their heads and turning them to one side. They will growl and if their opponent does not back down, they will charge, using their horns to create as big a clash as possible. Whilst brain injury is infrequent, broken necks can happen. More usually, injury is caused to the head, neck and horns.

Genetic Throwbacks

The sheep has a completely brown face. Occasionally paler rings around the eye, known as 'spectacles', will occur, and it is thought that this is a throwback to cross-breeding with a Castlemilk Morrit ram in 1936 and a Soay ram in 1966 when Manx Loaghtan stocks were low. This cross-breeding has resulted in some 'mouflon' markings in their descendants, including paler underbelly and tail, and sometimes a lighter patch under the chin.

Lambing up to 14 years old

The sheep are long-legged and thinly boned, being brown all over. They are small sheep with short tails, preferably with woolly tips. Ewes weigh in the region of 40kg, whilst rams are 55kg. The sheep are extremely hardy and require minimal additional feed. They are rarely affected by flystrike, footrot or gastro-intestinal worms. Ewes continue lambing up to the ages of 13–14 years. Depending on the level of additional care, lambing percentages range from 130–170 per cent with small and energetic offspring.

PORTLAND

- The origin of the Portland sheep is not altogether certain. That is because they have distinct differences between other primitive breeds in Britain.
- The Shetland, Manx and Soay sheep have short tails and are smaller – a trait common in Northern Short-tailed primitives, whilst the Portland sheep can breed out of season and have long tails – similar to Mediterranean breeds.
- They were kept in isolation on the Isle of Portland off the coast of Dorset, whilst the rest of Britain was experiencing a thriving wool trade by the time the Romans arrived.
- The invention of dyeing wool meant that white fleeces were in high demand, which created a practice of selection and cross-breeding. Primitive sheep lost their original characteristics.
- The Portland sheep was exonerated from this. Lambs born to the Portland still retain their original colouring, which indicate it is nearer its primitive state than other breeds.

Northern Short-tailed v Roman

The origin of the Portland sheep is not altogether certain. That is because they have distinct differences from other primitive breeds in Britain. The Shetland, Manx and Soay sheep have short tails and are smaller – a trait common in Northern Short-tailed primitives, whilst the Portland sheep can breed out of season and have long tails – similar to Mediterranean breeds. This would suggest that the Portland derives its origin from the Roman invasion of Britain. However it shares many similarities to the old

Jon D

tan-faced, horned sheep that were common in the south-west long before the Romans arrived.

Exonerated from the Thriving Wool Trade

The other factor to consider when discussing the origin of the Portland sheep is their location. They were kept in isolation on the Isle of Portland off the coast of Dorset, whilst the rest of Britain was experiencing a thriving wool trade by the time the Romans arrived. The invention of dyeing wool meant that white fleeces were in high demand, which created a practice of selection and cross-breeding. Primitive sheep lost their original characteristics. The Portland sheep was exonerated from this. Lambs born to the Portland still retain their original colouring, which indicate it is nearer its primitive state than other breeds. However, the Romans did bring with them Mediterranean sheep which they cross-bred with indigenous breeds, which may have found their way onto the Isle of Portland.

Bartering with the Dorset Markets

William the Conqueror took over the manor in Portland and continued the feudal Saxon practice of giving strips of land to tenants along with certain common land. Sheep were brought in at night, to amass manure for the arable crops. Meat was less valued than wool. Cheese was made from the sheep's milk. The wool and cheese was used to settle the tithes and to barter with Dorset markets. In 1299, according to the Doomsday Book, there were 900 sheep on the Isle of Portland.

Last Sheep on the Island

In 1840, four flocks, totalling 1,000 sheep were recorded on the island. A flock had been inaugurated on the mainland, at Calke Abbey in Derbyshire in 1770. However, in Portland, large amounts of farm and common land were bought for the creation of a breakwater around the harbour in 1847. This led to a rapid decrease in the flocks of Portland sheep during the following century, especially as demand was for bigger carcasses. The last sheep left the island in 1920 for auction in Dorchester where they were not in high demand.

Return to the Island

The breed edged on extinction and the RBST managed to trace the last few sheep and in 1974 it was found 86 breeding ewes still survived. There were three predominant bloodlines – Field/Marsden, Stubbs/Clutton and Harpur Crewe. Cyclic crossing and line breeding meant that by 1996 the breed was more secure. In 1977 a flock was reintroduced to the Isle of Portland at the request of the Portland Field Research Group and this flock was later acquired by Portland Prison.

Meat favoured by George III

The breed is hardy and thrifty, well suited to sparse grazing. They are small animals which usually only produce one lamb at any time of the year. Rams weigh in the region of 55kg, whilst ewes are 35–40kg. When lambs are produced they have a foxy red coat, which will become creamy white in the first few months. The sheep's face is tan but may be lighter around the eyes and muzzle. Both sexes have pale horns sometimes with a black line running through them. The rams' horns are heavily spiralled whilst the ewes' curve in a semi-circle. Lambs are considered too small to eat, so the sheep is taken to hogget and mutton. It is a delicious meat, with a fine texture and superb flavour, favoured by George III. Fleece weight is 2–3kg, with a staple length of 6–9cm and a quality of 50–60s.

SOAY

- The Soay sheep is named after the 100-hectare (250 acre) island of Soay in the St Kilda group situated around 65 km from North Uist in the Western Isles of Scotland.
- The sheep are thought to have been on that island since Viking times, as Soay is the word for 'sheep island' in Norse.
- 107 sheep were established on the island of Hirta in 1932, after the human population and their domestic sheep had all left.
- These sheep were allowed to live in feral conditions and in the 1950s they became the subject of scientific research looking into evolution, population dynamics and demography.
- Soay sheep have been chosen by Butser Ancient Farm in the South Downs, to function in exploratory excavation and analysis at their archaeology dig.
- Soay meat is lean with low cholesterol. It has a distinct gamey flavour and can command a premium price.

Viking Sheep

The Soay sheep is named after the 100-hectare island of Soay in the St Kilda group situated around 65 km from North Uist in the Western Isles of Scotland. It belongs to the Northern European Short-tailed breeds of sheep and looks like one of the most primitive members of that group. It is thought to have been on that island since Viking times, since Soay is the word for 'sheep island' in Norse. Its appearance is very alike the feral fore-bearers of agricultural sheep – the wild Mouflon of Corsica, Sardinia and Cyprus and the small-horned and long-legged Urial sheep native to Central Asia. Its feral nature means that it is amazingly agile and hardy, but much smaller than domesticated animals.

Scientific Island of Research

A number of Soay sheep were taken to Woburn Abbey by the Duke of Bedford in 1910 to establish an unusual and eye-catching flock. In 1932, 107 sheep were established on the island of Hirta, after the human population and their domestic sheep had all left. This was instigated by the Marquess of Bute. These sheep were allowed to live in feral conditions and in the 1950s they became the subject of scientific research looking into evolution, population dynamics and demography, which was ideal as the flock is closed and does not suffer from competition or predators.

John Green

Population Growth and Crashes

The island has a certain carrying capacity, which creates a population growth and subsequent crash, with the cycle repeating itself. It has been found that rams suffer most from adverse weather in winter, as they are exhausted from the autumn mating season. Ewes will have spent all summer grazing so they are in good shape, but they can suffer from bad weather in January and February when they are heavily pregnant and extensive rain causes a chill.

Archaeological Analysis

Other Soay sheep were exported by Martin Coles Harman from St Kilda to Lundy Island situated in Bristol Channel, after he bought the island in 1924. Soay sheep have been chosen by Butser Ancient Farm in the South Downs, to function at their archaeological dig, as they are so similar to ancient sheep. Some feral Soay sheep can be found in Somerset at Cheddar Gorge. All in all, numbers are up, and 1,500 sheep are alive and well on the island of St Hilda alone.

Small Lambs, Easy to Rise

Not surprisingly, the Soay sheep is incredibly hardy and able to survive even the worst weather. They seem to have a good resistance to footrot and flystrike – common ailments that affect sheep. They can lamb even at 10–12 years of age, although their lambing percentage is low: 80–90 per cent when they are feral, but climbing to 150 per cent in lowland conditions with good management. Lambs are small, but easy to rise.

Mouflon Markings

The Soay sheep is fine-boned with prominent withers. Rams weigh 40kg, whilst ewes are around 25kg. They are generally brown, ranging from tan to chocolate with mouflon markings, which involve white undersides, white rumps and sometimes a white chin. Occasionally a self-coloured sheep will occur, either being black or tan with no markings. Their fleece is shed naturally and is exceptionally fine although it does contain some coarse hairs. It is sought after by hand knitters, and has a staple length of 5–15cm, a fleece weight of 1.5–2.25kg and a quality of 44s–50s.

Premium Price for Gamey Meat

Soay meat is lean with low cholesterol. It has a distinct gamey flavour and can command a premium price. Soay sheep can be crossed with bigger sheep such as the Suffolk to create a larger carcass which will retain the lean, gamey taste. Soay lambs are rarely slaughtered as they lack size and the sheep is generally used as hogget or mutton. A carcass of about 15kg can be expected at a year old. The Wiltshire Wildlife Trust have a flock of ¾ Wiltshire Horn, ¼ Soay ewes which they breed with the Southdown to create a sheep that can survive in very thrifty conditions.

TEESWATER

- It is said that when the Romans invaded Britain, they came with flocks of large, longwool sheep which they distributed all over the country.
- These in time evolved into varying breeds taking their name after the region in which they had differentiated, such as the Cotswolds, Lincoln, Leicester and Teeswater.
- The predominant use for the Teeswater is in crossing with a hill sheep to create the Masham lamb, which has the best attributes of the Teeswater, with a long, well-formed carcass, prolific lambing with excellent milking and maternal instincts.
- With good management Teeswaters can reach a lambing percentage of 250 per cent. Realistically a lambing percentage of 200 per cent is the ideal as ewes struggle to rear more than two lambs.

Original Roman Flocks

It is said that when the Romans invaded Britain, they came with flocks of large, longwool sheep which they distributed all over the country. These in time evolved into varying breeds taking their name after the region in which they had differentiated, such as the Cotswolds, Lincoln and Leicester. At the

Peakman

time, all these sheep would have been white-faced, and it is thought that the Teeswater would have been developed from one of these original Roman flocks.

A Resurgence after the Second World War

Although the breed was improved during the nineteenth century it still was fairly concentrated in the Tees Valley in County Durham. Numbers were falling and by the 1920s the breed was becoming very rare. However, since the end of the Second World War the sheep have enjoyed a resurgence. The Teeswater Sheep Breeders' Association (TSBA) was created in 1949 with the aim of improving the breeding of the sheep to preserve their pedigree and also to maintain the dominance of the Teeswater in crossing with hill sheep.

Masham Half-Bred

Hill sheep include the Dalesbred, Swaledale, Rough Fell, Scottish Blackface and Exmoor Horn. These ewes, when crossed with a Teeswater or Wensleydale ram, produce a cross-bred ewe known as a Masham, which has the best characteristics of the ram's breed, with a long, well-formed carcass, prolific lambing with good milking and maternal instincts. Continental sires, such as the Rouge, Bleu de Maine, Texel and Charolais cannot produce a Masham as unlike the Teeswater and Wensleydale they don't have the fleece quality. They can however be used be used as terminal sires on Masham ewes to produce good commercial lambs. The Mule, which is usually a mixture of a Bluefaced Leicester ram and a mountain ewe, is the most popular half breed. Like the Masham, it performs well in both upland and lowland areas.

Lambing Percentage of 250 per cent

The predominant use for the Teeswater is in crossing with a hill sheep to create the Masham lamb. However it is also raised as purebred for the production of meat. The Teeswater is lean, with muscular hindquarters. Lambs attain a weight of 19.9kg by eight weeks old, and their meat is still lean when they are taken up to a deadweight of 30kg. Wool is used by handspinners and it is long, very fine and kemp free. It has a staple length of 20–30cm, a weight of 4–6kg and a quality of 32s–36s. Ewes weigh 90kg, whilst rams are 120kg. They have dark colouration on the nose and ear areas on a white/grey face. The sheep do well in most conditions and lamb until 10–12 years of age. With good management they can reach a lambing percentage of 250 per cent with medium sized lambs which are fast developers. Realistically a lambing percentage of 200 per cent is the ideal as ewes struggle to rear more than two lambs.

WENSLEYDALE

- They are unique among breeds in that they can trace their development back to the original sire.
- Richard Outhaite of East Appleton, near Bedale in North Yorkshire, paid a total of 40 guineas in 1838 to use a renowned Dishley Leicester ram on his Muggs (a now extinct longwool sheep which bore similarities to the Teeswater).
- Out of the lambs produced, in 1839, was the legendary Blue Cap, a ram who grew to 32 stone (more than 200kg).
- It was not until 1876, when the Yorkshire Show needed a reference for the sheep in order to enter it into classes, that a name was given to these sheep.
- The sheep has been reported by the British Meat and Livestock Commission as 'probably the heaviest of all our indigenous breeds'.
- The Wensleydale is often used as a crossing sire with hill ewes, conveying bulk, conformation and fertility onto the resultant lambs.

Exact Origins

These sheep originated in the Yorkshire Dales. They are unique among breeds in that they can trace their development back to the original sire which was a renowned Dishley Leicester owned by Mr Sonley of Lund Court, Kirbymoorside. Richard Outhaite of East Appleton, near Bedale in North Yorkshire, paid a total of 40 guineas in 1838 to use the ram on his Muggs (a now extinct longwool sheep which bore similarities to the Teeswater). Out of the lambs produced, in 1839, was the legendary Blue Cap, a ram who grew to 32 stone (more than 200kg). His face was deep blue and he had black skin covered in beautifully fine, white wool. His progeny invariably shared the same characteristics.

The Yorkshire Show needs a Name

It was not until 1876, when the Yorkshire Show needed a reference for the sheep in order to enter it into classes, that a name was given to these sheep. In 1890 two breed societies were formed, each with different and divergent interests. By 1920 it was felt that it would be in both their interest to amalgamate and the present-day Wensleydale Longwool Sheep Breeders' Association was formed.

Big Lambs

The sheep has been reported by the British Meat and Livestock Commission as 'probably the heaviest of all our indigenous breeds'. Ewes weigh 90kg and rams 135kg. Lambs are big, weighing 6kg as twins or 8kg on their own. A

lambing percentage of 250 per cent can be attained although 175–200 per cent is normal. Bigger lambs can result in birthing problems.

Lean Meat

The Wensleydale is often used as a crossing sire with hill ewes, conveying bulk, conformation and fertility onto the resultant lambs which is particularly useful for the lowland farmer. It has been shown that although the Wensleydale crosses do not develop as fast as Down crosses, the lambs are a lot leaner when slaughtered at greater weights.

Quality Forelock

The breed has a characteristic long body with a deep chest and dark-skinned face free from wool, except for a forelock of wool known as the 'topping'. This forelock is said to have been fashioned so that the quality of the fleece could be easily examined. The impressive fleece is long and curling. It reaches a staple length of 20–25cm, with a fleece weight of 4.5–6kg and quality of 44s–48s.

MINORITY (1,500 TO 3,000)

BALWEN

- The Balwen means 'white blaze' in Welsh, stemming from the word 'bal', meaning 'blaze' and 'wen' for 'white'.
- It was the custom in Wales for farmers to breed sheep with very distinctive markings so that they could pinpoint them easily on the mountain.
- The Balwen were originally found in a very isolated area of the Upper Tywi Valley covering approximately 50 square miles on the periphery of Carmarthenshire and Breconshire.
- Their isolated environment made them very vulnerable to extinction and when the severe winter of 1946–7 struck, the sheep suffered terribly and there was only one ram remaining.
- Other pressures, such as the increased planting of coniferous forests pushed them out.

White Blaze

The Balwen means 'white blaze' in Welsh, stemming from the word 'bal', meaning 'blaze' and 'wen' for 'white'. The sheep are ideally black but can also be seen in dark brown or grey. They have a characteristic white blaze on the face, with a black nose and four white socks. The tip of their tail is white. Rams are horned, whereas ewes are polled. It was the custom in Wales for farmers to breed sheep with very distinctive markings so that they could pinpoint them easily on the mountain.

Isolated Danger

Over the centuries, through selective breeding, native Welsh Mountain Sheep have evolved into many different types, but they all come under the banner of Welsh Mountain Sheep. The Balwen were originally found in a very isolated area of the Upper Tywi Valley covering approximately 50 square miles on the periphery of Carmarthenshire and Breconshire. They were first recorded over 80 years ago but were thought to have been there for at least 150 years. Their isolated environment made them very vulnerable to extinction and when

the severe winter of 1946–7 struck, the sheep suffered terribly and the flock was left with only one ram remaining. Other pressures, such as the increased planting of coniferous forests pushed them out. However, numbers did grow throughout the 1950s and 1960s as people in the valley tried to save them and by the 1970s the world outside the Tywi Valley began to take notice. The Balwen Welsh Mountain Breed Society was created in 1985, and the breed is now widespread and popular with both smallholders and farmers.

More Food, More Lambs

The breed is hardy and able to cope with severe weather and little grazing. Farmers say that they have a good resistance to footrot and flystrike. Ewes have the ability to lamb until they are 10 years of age, with a lambing percentage of 100 per cent on the uplands, although this can increase to up to 200 per cent on the lowlands. A lamb will produce a small carcass, although it does not need extra feed, and can be predicted to reach a weight of 12–14kg at 16 weeks, similar to other Welsh Mountain breeds. If a larger carcass is required, a suitable terminal sire can produce a bigger lamb. If using a Balwen ram to sire a cross-bred lamb with a commercial ewe who has not lambed before you can expect a smaller, energetic lamb ensuring an easy first-time birth.

DEVON CLOSEWOOL

- The Devon Closewool was bred in the mid-1800s, the result of a cross between the Exmoor Horn sheep and the Devon Longwool.
- It proved very popular and by 1950 there were 229,000 registered sheep in the country – the most populous bred of that time, primarily based in Devon.
- The RBST took a flock to Suffolk in 2015 to reduce the threat of it being too geographically concentrated.
- The sheep has been bred for the climatic conditions of Exmoor, which include the insistent Atlantic rain, and can thrive where other breeds would not.
- The thick, average length, strong stapled fleece is what enables the sheep to cope with dense rain on the hill.
- The sheep is perfect for the first-timer, being docile and easily managed.

Popular but too Geographically Concentrated

The Devon Closewool was bred in the mid-1800s, the result of a cross between the Exmoor Horn sheep and the Devon Longwool. It proved very popular and by 1950 there were 229,000 registered sheep in the country – the most populous bred of that time, primarily based in Devon. The Devon Closewool Sheep Breeders' Society was inaugurated in 1923. Although the breed is now spread further afield, the RBST did take a flock to Suffolk in 2015 to reduce the threat of it being too geographically concentrated. A number of sheep were taken to Canada in 1947, and there have also been exports to New Zealand. The sheep has been bred for the climatic conditions of Exmoor, which include the insistent Atlantic rain, and can thrive where other breeds would not.

Flourishing Half-Breeds

When a Devon Closewool is mated to a Continental sheep or Down it produces half-bred lambs which finish early, gaining weight rapidly, without needing additional feeding. Closewool rams develop hardiness and solidity when used to upgrade other white-faced breeds. Halfbred lambs created from a cross with a Closewool ewe and either a Border Leicester, Bluefaced Leicester, Suffolk or Texel ram are renowned for their capacity to flourish in different climates and farming structures. The halfbred ewes are strong, with superb milking abilities, able to care for twins on grassland up to 1,100 feet above sea

level. If this halfbred ewe is further crossed with a terminal variety she will generally have a lambing percentage of 180–200 per cent in a lowland flock.

Delicious, Well Marbled Meat

Purebred sheep attain a deadweight of 18–21kg in 12–16 weeks on a forage diet. On the hill, lambs reach the same weight in 20–24 weeks, producing a delicious, well marbled meat. The fleece weight in rams is 6kg, whilst ewes are 4kg. The thick, average length, strong stapled fleece is what enables the sheep to cope with dense rain on the hill. It has a quality of 48–53s, with a fleece weight of 2.25–3kg and a staple length of 8–10cm. The sheep is predominantly kept for meat.

Perfect for the First Timer

The sheep is perfect for the first-timer, being docile and easily managed. Both sexes are polled. Lambing percentages range from 150–170 per cent and ewes will continue lambing for seven yields, whilst rams perform for six to seven years. A farmer looking for an easy to manage, low maintenance sheep that flourishes on a grass system, will also like this sheep. It is a very solid looking breed, with black nostrils and short ears that are covered with dense white hair. They keep their teeth well. A short neck, and thick, well set shoulders lead to a broad back, with a well let down leg of mutton. Ewes weigh 60–62kg and rams 100kg.

DORSET DOWN

- The Dorset Down originated from the early 1800s when local Hampshire, Berkshire and Wiltshire ewes were crossed with Southdown rams.
- The breed society was created in 1904, with the breed enjoying much popularity throughout the first 50 years of the twentieth century.
- However, Continental breeds, such as the Texel and the huge commerciality of the Suffolk, pushed the Dorset Downs to the fringes of the market with dramatically falling numbers.
- The Dorset Down ram is incredibly virile and has such a high pheromone count that they are often used as teasers.
- They can work at any time of year and can serve 20 ewes in 24 hours, habitually being put to 40 or 50 ewes at one time.

Wonderful Terminal Ram

The Dorset Down originated from the early 1800s when local Hampshire, Berkshire and Wiltshire ewes were crossed with Southdown rams. It is not related to the white-faced Dorset Horn. Over time, the Dorset Down became renowned as a wonderful terminal ram. The breed society was created in 1904, with the breed enjoying much popularity throughout the first 50 years of the twentieth century. However, Continental breeds, such as the Texel and the hugely commercial Suffolk, pushed the Dorset Downs to the fringes of the market with dramatically falling numbers. In contrast to other Down breeds, which have gained a foothold in the market, (in the 1980s, 43 per cent of ewes in the UK were put to a 'Down' ram), the Dorset Down has never recovered.

Incredible Virile Rams

This is unusual as the Dorset Down ram is incredibly virile and has such a high pheromone count that they are often used as teasers. They can work at any time of year and can serve 20 ewes in 24 hours, habitually being put to 40 or 50 ewes at one time. Lambs produced are fast growing on grass, and research has shown that they match Suffolk crosses regarding grading of meat. Lambs are produced with small heads and shoulders and therefore ewes have few lambing problems. As a result, the Dorset Down ram can be used on primitive breeds such as the Manx Loaghtan or Soay. When used on hill sheep they improve conformation. The Dorset Down ewe will take the ram throughout the majority of the year.

Meat and Wool

In terms of meat, a single purebred lamb will achieve a dressed carcass weight of 18kg by 10–12 weeks. It will take twin lambs 12–14 weeks to reach this weight. The fleece is short, with fine fibres closely packed to protect the sheep from wet weather. Fleeces weigh up to 2.5kg greasy and 2.2kg washed. They have a staple length of 5–8cm and a quality of 56s–58s, making them suitable for the hosiery trade.

Easily Trained to the Bucket

The sheep is substantial and stocky, and although able to weather most situations, is not appropriate for uplands. Like other Downs breeds it is docile and easily trained to the bucket. Ewes achieve a lambing percentage of 150 per cent. They weigh 70kg and rams 110kg. It is comparable in looks to the Hampshire Down sheep with its deep brown, wool-free head and lack of horns in both sexes.

GREYFACE DARTMOOR

- They originate from ancient stock that historically were found over Dartmoor, in Devon.
- In the nineteenth century local Longwool breeds were bought in to attempt to breed the Dartmoor into a more marketable sheep.
- They were successful, as Greyface Dartmoor are now found throughout England, Wales, the south of Scotland and Ireland, although the majority are kept in small flocks.
- The Greyface Dartmoor ewes do not have such a high lambing percentage as other longwools, but their progeny is hardier and thriftier, grading well and maturing fast.
- They possess a weighty, adaptable fleece, appropriate for use in carpets, blankets and various hard-wearing commodities.

Ancient Stock

This breed is also called the Dartmoor or Improved Dartmoor. They originate from ancient stock that historically were found on Dartmoor, in Devon. In the nineteenth century local Longwool breeds were bought in to attempt to develop the Dartmoor into a more marketable sheep. By 1909, the Dartmoor Sheep Breeders' Association had been formed to regulate, market and develop the breed, which had strong affiliation with the regions of South Hams, Chagford and Tavistock in Devon. They were successful, as Greyface Dartmoor are now found throughout England, Wales, the south of Scotland and Ireland, although the majority are kept in small flocks. Greyface Dartmoor have also been exported for breeding overseas.

Hardy, Thrifty Lambs

The Greyface Dartmoor ewes are wonderful mothers and can be crossed with a terminal sire to yield a quality commercial lamb. The Greyface Dartmoor ewes do not have such a high lambing percentage as other longwools, but their progeny is hardier and thriftier, grading well and maturing fast. Purebred lambs attain 16–20kg deadweight at four months, with the sheep being lean enough to take on to greater weights i.e. 20–30kg at eight to nine months.

Valuable Fleece

They possess a weighty, adaptable fleece, appropriate for use in carpets,

blankets and various hard-wearing commodities. Although the breed is predominantly raised for meat, there is money to be made from its fleece. Fleece weight is 7–9kg, staple length is 25–30cm and quality is 36s–40s.

Characteristic Black Speckling on their Nose

Greyface Dartmoor are calm sheep and straightforward to bucket train. Footrot does not seem to be a problem. They produce small, energetic lambs with little difficulty in giving birth, attaining a lambing percentage of 150 per cent. Ewes weigh 60–70kg, whilst rams are 75–100kg. They are a longwool breed, with lengthy, curly wool that covers every area of their body, apart from their face. They have characteristic black or grey spotting or speckling on their nose, feet and occasionally their ears. Rams can sometimes have horns.

LLANWENOG

- The Llanwenog is a medium-sized breed developed in the late nineteenth century by crossing the Shropshire Down sheep to local black-faced breeds in west Wales, primarily in the Teifi Valley, such as the now extinct Llanllwni, Welsh Mountain and Clun Forest sheep.
- When a rail link was established from Shrewsbury into Cardiganshire and further to Carmarthen in 1867, local Welsh landowners purchased flocks of the Shropshire Down and began improving their local sheep.
- The Second World War played havoc with the breed's uniformity as the need for food production was paramount and extensive outcrossing with larger breeds occurred.
- In 1972 the Meat and Livestock Commission documented that in that year they were the only the British breed that were achieving a lambing percentage of greater than 200 per cent.

Railway Opens up Wales

The Llanwenog is a medium-sized breed developed in the late nineteenth century by crossing the Shropshire Down sheep to local black-faced breeds in west Wales, primarily in the Teifi Valley, such as the now extinct Llanllwni, Welsh Mountain and Clun Forest sheep. The Shropshire Down was well known for its profligacy and wonderful wool and meat, which were sold at large sales in Shrewsbury. When a rail link was established from Shrewsbury into Cardiganshire and further to Carmarthen in 1867, local Welsh landowners purchased flocks of the Shropshire Down and began improving their local sheep. By the 1930s these Shropshire crosses or Blackfaces, as they were called, were common throughout west Wales.

Trophies for Lambing

The Second World War played havoc with the breed's uniformity as the need for food production was paramount and extensive outcrossing with larger breeds occurred. In 1957, the Llanwenog Sheep Society, named after the region where most of the sheep lived, was created with the aim of stabilising and marketing the breed, which had some remarkable attributes. One of these was profligacy, with the breed gaining trophies throughout the 1960s at national lambing competitions. The highlight came in 1972 when the Meat and Livestock Commission documented that in that year they were the only

British breed that were achieving a lambing percentage of greater than 200 per cent. Although still concentrated in west Wales, the breed is a presence in the show ring throughout England and Wales.

Popular in Farm Shops

A lambing percentage of 200 per cent can be reached with a good management on a lowland flock, although 180 per cent is more common. The ewe produces small lambs with little complications. These lambs grow well, with weights of 15.2kg at eight weeks, and can be slaughtered at 4–5 months with a deadweight of 16–18kg. When mated with a terminal sire the resultant lambs will attain larger weights with superior grades. Llanwenog meat is well-liked by farm shops and is highly marketable. Rams can attain a weight of 90kg and ewes 55kg.

Distinctive Tuft

Llanwenogs have a good conformation, with black faces and legs, bulky white fleece, and a distinctive tuft of wool on the forehead. They have a staple length of 6–10cm, a fleece weight of 2–2.5kg and quality of 50s–56s. Neither rams or ewes have horns. They are placid sheep, inexpensive to feed and can be housed in bad weather.

Norfolk Horn

- The Norfolk Horn is an ancient breed of British sheep, tracing its roots back to the Saxon black-faced sheep once common throughout Northern Europe.
- The sheep flourishes in dry, cold weather on meagre vegetation – conditions where other breeds would lose fitness.
- In the late eighteenth century, when sheep crossing became all the rage, the Norfolk was scorned by local farmers who did not value the breed.
- The Suffolk sheep was created from the frequent cross between the Norfolk Horn and the Southdown sheep.
- The Suffolk is the most popular choice with farmers today, who use the rams to produce finished lambs. The Norfolk Horn has therefore been an important asset to modern British farming.
- The last remaining purebred ram died in 1973.

Scorned by Farmers

The Norfolk Horn is an ancient breed of British sheep, tracing its roots back to the Saxon black-faced sheep once common throughout Northern Europe. It developed in East Anglia – throughout Norfolk, Suffolk, north Essex and south east Cambridgeshire. The breed is adapted to thrive on poor forage such as found on the heathland regions, like Breckland in north west Norfolk. Prior to the late 1700s, no-one really considered selectively breeding and improving sheep, but in the late eighteenth century, when sheep crossing became all the rage, the Norfolk was scorned by local farmers who did not value the breed. The superb quality of its meat, however, did not go unrecognised. The Southdown was introduced into the area, with the aim of replacing the Norfolk Horn. Crosses between these two breeds became frequent and it was from this blend that the Suffolk sheep was formed, with its own society being created in 1886. The Suffolk is the most popular choice with farmers today, who use the rams to produce finished lambs. The Norfolk Horn has therefore been an important asset to modern British farming.

Backcrossing to Revive the Breed

The population of Norfolk Horns fell, with extinction imminent at the turn of the twentieth century. After the First World War, in 1919, Mr J.D. Sayer kept the last remaining flock, which he had developed since 1895. He shared these

sheep in the 1940s and 50s with the Cambridge Animal Research Station, who were investigating inbreeding through the passing on of cryptorchidism (the lack of one or both testes from the scrotum). Towards the end of the 1960s only a few, terribly inbred sheep were left. These were handed onto Whipsnade Park and from there, the National Agricultural Centre. The last remaining purebred ram died in 1973. A series of back-crossing breeding, using the Suffolk, Swaledale, Wiltshire Horn and Llanwenog rams, were used on Norfolk Horn ewes to create sheep that were over 90 per cent, or 15/16 Norfolk Horn. Since the 1970s Norfolk Horn numbers have risen considerably, and although they remain rare, they are no longer in danger of extinction, although with few blood lines, inbreeding is still an issue.

Cross-breeding Excellence

The sheep flourishes in dry, cold weather on meagre vegetation – conditions where other breeds would lose fitness. Lambing percentages are high: 170 per cent is expected. The breed is long-legged and narrow. Both sexes have heavy horns, which spiral, but should not grow into the face or head. Rams are more strongly horned than the ewes. Norfolk horn sheep have black heads and faces, which should be without wool. Their fleece is dense and white. Newborn lambs possess a dark or mottled fleece which turns white as they mature; however a few black spots are allowed in the adult. Ewes weigh 70kg, rams 90–95kg. As has been shown with the Suffolk, the Norfolk Horn is useful for cross-breeding. Purebred lambs attain 17–18kg deadweight on a grass system by five months and the meat contains little fat, so that the lambs are appropriate to take to a heavier weight. The meat is delicious and perfect for direct marketing. Staple length is 7–10cm, fleece weight 1–1.5kg and quality 54s–56s

OXFORD DOWN

- The Oxford Down was developed in the 1830s by breeding Cotswold rams with Southdown and Hampshire ewes.
- The majority of the preliminary flocks were centred around the market town of Witney in Oxfordshire and so the sheep were named accordingly.
- The breed was widely sought after and was exported to Argentina, Russia, the US, Canada and Europe.
- It was the primary choice as a crossing sire throughout the first half of the twentieth century.
- This popularity did not last. Between 1955 and 1970 butchers were focusing on smaller breeds, as the public wanted smaller joints. The Suffolk and imported Texel gained favour over Down breeds.
- The Oxford Down is the heaviest of all Down breeds with the weightiest fleece.

Primary Crossing Sire in the UK

The Oxford Down was developed in the 1830s by breeding Cotswold rams with Southdown and Hampshire ewes. The majority of the preliminary flocks were centred around the market town of Witney in Oxfordshire and so the sheep were named accordingly. The Oxford Down Sheep Breeders' Association was formed in 1889, publishing the first flock book that year. The breed was widely sought after and was exported to Argentina, Russia, the US, Canada and Europe. It was the primary choice as a crossing sire throughout the first half of the twentieth century. In the region of 1,000 rams were sold every year at the Kelso Rams' Sales in the Scottish Borders. This popularity did not last. Between 1955 and 1970 butchers were focusing on smaller breeds, as the public wanted smaller joints. The Suffolk and imported Texel gained favour over Down breeds, but handfuls of enthusiasts across the country – from the Midlands, to Yorkshire, Eire, Aberdeenshire, Northumberland and the Borders

Yew Tree registered flock

– continued caring for their sheep during the 1970s, and they were rewarded in the 1980s when the rams began to be used as a crossing sire again.

Heaviest of all Down Breeds

The Oxford Down is an extremely large, robust sheep that shares the good makeup of Downs breeds. Ewes weigh in the region of 90kg, whilst rams are 120–140kg, distinguishing it as the heaviest of all Downs breeds. They have a thick, white fleece complete with a top-knot. Their fleece is the weightiest in the Downs category. It is used for hosiery, felt-making and knitting, with a staple length of 10–15cm, weight of 3–4kg and quality of 50s–54s. The legs and face of the Oxford Down are dark brown. The legs are woolly, whilst the face is not. Neither sex possesses horns.

Lean Lambs

The Oxford Down ram can create early maturing, heavy, lean lambs using ewes from the majority of breeds. These lambs can be killed at twelve weeks. Cross-bred lambs can also be taken to increased weights, even hogget weights, whilst still retaining leanness. The Oxford Down ram has achieved a specialist role as a terminal sire. A purebred Oxford Down will attain 22.4kg when eight weeks old, reaching a deadweight of 18–22kg, with good marbled meat, at 3–4 months. Purebred lambs are sold at premium markets such as Farmers' Markets and private butchers.

CATTLE

CRITICAL
(FEWER THAN 150 BREEDING FEMALES)

Chillingham Wild Cattle
Dairy Shorthorn (Original Population)
Northern Dairy Shorthorn
Vaynol

ENDANGERED
(150 TO 250)

Native Aberdeen Angus
Whitebred Shorthorn

VULNERABLE
(250 TO 450)

Lincoln Red (Original Population)

AT RISK
(450 TO 750)

Gloucester

MINORITY
(750 TO 1,500)

British White
Irish Moiled
Shetland
Traditional Hereford
White Park

CRITICAL (FEWER THAN 150)

CHILLINGHAM WILD CATTLE

- The cattle were kept for sport. They were hunted on horseback with packs of dogs and spears or swords.
- The cattle's aggressive nature and dangerous horns made the hunt all the more exciting.
- Twenty Chillingham Wild Cattle were removed from the herd amid biosecurity concerns a few years ago.
- A cow can come into season at any time – they do not have a set rutting time. This means the bulls are constantly competing for a chance to mate.
- Inbreeding is as such that newly born animals are practically genetically identical. This incredibly rare state of affairs comes about because they receive the same genes from both their mother and their father.

History

If you go back a few hundred years, wild cattle would have been a common sight throughout Britain. In the early 1900s only four truly wild herds were left. The Chillingham Wild Cattle are some of the last remaining survivors of the ancient herds that used to roam Britain's forests. The herd was first recorded at Chillingham Castle in 1645, and they have been there ever since.

Totally wild

At first, they were used to defend the castle. These amazing animals are totally wild. Even today, they are not inspected by vets. They have never been touched by a human. Viewing the cattle has to be done with the help of a warden. There is a lot of respect for the cattle. There are no passports, ear tagging, castration or worming. They do not feature on any cattle database. The only human intervention is the giving of a little hay if they cannot access grass during a particularly cold winter. Otherwise they are wild, and potentially dangerous creatures.

Ancestry

Both Charles Darwin and Sir David Attenborough have inspected the herd. Originally it was thought that they descended from the aurochs – oxen who

roamed the earth during prehistoric times. Later thinking, due to their small size, pointed at ancestors from the Neolithic era, when farmers would use the oxen to aid in their work.

Chillingworth Castle

The cattle are thought to have been on the estate of Chillingham Castle since the 1300s. The Castle is a former monastery situated 10 miles from the sea, between Berwick-upon-Tweed and Alnwick. It has beautiful views across Northumberland and the Cheviots. It is home to a large variety of British wildlife, including Fallow and Roe deer, brown hares, foxes, badgers and the native red squirrel. The ancient beech and oak trees are home to over 50 species of birds.

Field Sport

It is thought that the cattle were kept for sport instead of dairy or meat produce. They were hunted on horseback with packs of dogs and spears or swords, much later with guns. The cattle's aggressive nature and dangerous horns, on both male and female cattle, would have made the hunt all the more exciting. The future King Edward VII killed the king bull in a hunting party in 1872.

Present Populations

The Chillingham Wild Cattle Association was formed in 1939 to protect these

beasts. They now own the park and the cattle. From 2009, the cattle were afforded 130ha in mainly woodland or farmland. As from January 2019, they number about 90 animals: 50 per cent bulls and 50 per cent cows. In 1946–7, during a particularly cold winter, there were only five bulls and eight cows remaining,

Biosecurity Fears

Twenty Chillingham Wild Cattle were removed from the herd to the Crown Estate situated near Fochabers in NE Scotland amid biosecurity concerns a few years ago. They now number about 30, and are a good insurance policy against disease, such as Foot and Mouth disease.

Meat

Since the cattle do not receive vaccinations or undergo TB tests, their meat, under any condition, is banned from the human food chain.

Characteristics

The Chillingham Wild Cattle are small. Bulls weigh in the region of 300kg, whilst cows are 280kg. Both genders have upright horns. They are white, but quite often have red colouring in their ears. This colour may also extend to their feet, nose and around the eyes. They have a primitive conformation as opposed to the White Park Cattle, which have a typical British beef conformation.

Mating in a smaller herd

When the herd was a lot smaller, it was dominated by one bull, who ruled supreme. He mated with all the cows and fought any younger bull who provoked him. After 2–3 years, he tired, and gave up his place as king bull, to a younger, more robust male.

Mating rituals now

With a larger herd, numbering 90, there are too many cows for just one mating bull, and too much competition from more vigorous bulls. So now, there are 6–8 dominant bulls, who will all compete and spar with each other to gain their place. When a cow comes in season, they will paw the earth rubbing their faces in the soil and giving off guttural, growling noises.

A bull is not expected to live more than 12 years. A cow can live to 15. Only the most powerful bulls get the opportunity to mate.

Fatalities during mating

In the years between 1945–2005 there were fatalities of 11 bulls and 3 cows who died of their injuries caused by other herd members.

Coming into Season

Similar to other bovines but unlike many large, wild species, the Chillingham Wild Cattle do not have a set rutting season. A cow can come into season at any time – all year round. That means that the bulls are constantly competing for a chance to mate. With around 45 females in the herd, you can expect half that number in calves per year. A cow can calve from three years old.

Birth

Cows take themselves off, away from the herd to give birth. They will leave the calf, returning only to feed it a twice a day, until it is a few days old and can follow her back to the herd. The herd will reject the calf if they think it is too weak. They will kill it or leave it to die. This increases the genetic strength of the herd.

Genetics

There has been some gene flow from the Chillingham Wild Cattle towards

the White Park Cattle in the early 1900s. This is not the case the other way around. This is shown by the Chillingham Wild Cattle's red ear colouration. The White Park has black ears, which is a dominant gene over red.

The link between the two breeds has not been fully researched, but historically, the Chillingham Wild Cattle would have probably been more similar to the Vaynol Cattle. Since they have never been selectively bred, they are considerably smaller than modern day cattle and do not share a lot of similar traits.

Homozygous Blood Groups

Studies in 1960 showed the Chillingham Wild Cattle to have homozygous blood groups, which is a result of their long years of inbreeding. Disease resistant genes were shown to be too similar to prevent widespread immunity from certain afflictions, but generally they have proven to have a very strong immunity.

Inbreeding is as such that newly born animals are practically genetically identical. This, incredibly rare state of affairs, comes about because they receive the same genes from both their mother and their father.

DAIRY SHORTHORN
(ORIGINAL POPULATION)

- The first herd book was published in 1822 and was made up of 710 bulls and 850 cows. It was the first recorded genealogy herd book for cattle.
- The Dairy Shorthorn cattle numbered amongst the original cattle sent to establish herds in Australia.
- It has served as a foundation stock for many breeds including the Illawarra cattle in Australia and the Swedish Red and Norwegian Red.
- Since the 1940s, the breed has become incredibly rare as requirements have changed in the cattle industry with intensification and specialisation.
- The Original Population is made up from pure bred cows born prior to 1958, which is when the herd book was divided into Dairy and Beef elements.

History

The Dairy Shorthorn originated in the North East of England in the late eighteenth century and was a cross between Teeswater and Durham cattle.

The first herd book was published in 1822 and was made up of 710 bulls and 850 cows. This herd book, known as *Coates's Herd Book* was the first recorded genealogy herd book for cattle breeds in the world. The Shorthorn Society of Great Britain and Ireland was created in 1874. They bought the copyright of the herd book and continued to compile and publish it ever since.

In the early twentieth century, this breed was principally used both for meat and milk – a dual purpose breed. It was so popular that during the 1930s and 1940s, two out of every three cows in the UK were a purebred Shorthorn or cross-bred Shorthorn. Indeed in 1937/8 the number of bulls registered with MAFF (who licensed all bulls) was 23,730 Dairy Shorthorn bulls to 12,917 bulls combining all other breeds. This popularity led to the Beef Shorthorn being registered in its own section of *Coate's Herd Book* in 1958, with Dairy having a separate division.

The 1970s saw an influx of cross-breeding with the original herd. The RBST are only concerned with the purebred type, which is prior to the herd book being split in 1958.

The Dairy Shorthorn cattle numbered amongst the original cattle sent to establish herds in Australia. 1783 saw the first Shorthorns being imported to the US, into Virginia and Maryland. By the 1800s, additional imports ensured the breed was widely available throughout the country. The Dairy Shorthorn was the first dairy cow to arrive in New Zealand, in 1814, with the cow gaining

popularity to become the predominant breed for many years.

Today, the Dairy Shorthorn is found all over the world – in the UK, Ireland, Australia, South Africa and in Canada, New Zealand and the US, where it is known as the Milking Shorthorn. It has served as a foundation stock for many breeds, including the Illawarra cattle found in Australia and the Swedish Red and Norwegian Red.

Characteristics

The cattle are long lived and fertile – cows can still calve at 14–17 years old. They are docile and easy to look after. Their colouration ranges from red, red with white markings, to white or roan, and a cow will weigh 550–650kg. Bulls weigh substantially more than that. Their shape is generally 'dairy' with less muscle than cattle bred especially for beef, but not quite as lean as modern day dairy herds. They do have horns, but these are often removed for easy handling.

Milk

Traditionally the cow is primarily used for milk. Although yields are not high, the Dairy Shorthorn goes on producing milk for years after a modern cow, giving much the same lifetime production, making them suitable for a low-input dairy operation. On average, 7,000kg of milk is produced by the Dairy Shorthorn every year over 305 days, with a 3.8 per cent butterfat content and 3.3 per cent protein.

Meat

The dual-purpose qualities of this breed are still evident. A bull calf can be effectively finished for beef, attaining good grades.

Genetics

Since the 1940s, the breed has become incredibly rare as requirements have changed in the cattle industry with intensification and specialisation. In 2015 an embryo transfer project was initiated, using surrogate mothers as well as storage in the RBST gene bank. Across the world, Dairy Shorthorn genes have been used to improve the dairy production of herds, resulting in 'blended' Shorthorns with varying levels of purity.

NORTHERN DAIRY SHORTHORN

- The Northern Dairy Shorthorn was developed as a dual-purpose cow, specifically for the uplands.
- In an average lactation of 305 days, the cow will produce 3,500 to 6,000 litres on a forage-based diet.
- The Northern Dairy Shorthorn can go on producing milk for 10 or more lactations.
- Due to the rarity of the breed, embryos were taken to implant into surrogate mothers. Embryos are also preserved at the RBST Gene Bank.

Ancestry

All cattle are thought to have descended from the wild Aurochs which lived in a reasonably small region of Europe, Western Asia and the northern most parts of Africa. These cattle have evolved through domestication, where different strains have been developed with various sizes, shapes, colouration, horns or polled, and most importantly, function. Cattle were bred specifically for milk, meat or their skin. Some were bred for two or more purposes and were known as dual purpose. These ancient, native breeds have a resistance to health problems that modern day cattle do not. Ancestors of the Northern Dairy Shorthorn are thought to have come over to the UK with the Vikings.

History

The Northern Dairy Shorthorn was developed as a dual-purpose cow, specifically for the uplands, where they could live, even in winter, with very

little care or expensive feed. Robert Bakewell and the two siblings, Charles and Robert Colling, worked in the Pennines and neighbouring areas of Durham and Westmorland in the late 1700s. They improved the Teeswater and Durham breeds to create the roan, red, or white cattle that had small, sweeping horns.

It took until 1944 for these animals to be registered as distinct from the Beef Shorthorn and Dairy Shorthorn. 1944 saw the registration of 750 bulls and 1,000 cows; however, with intensive farming using specialist breeds, numbers fell dramatically. In 1969, it was recorded in *Coates Herd Book* amongst the additional Shorthorns. Today, there are a small amount of breeders keeping the pedigree breed alive but they suffer from a small number of purebred breeding females.

Characteristics

Females can breed until 14–17 years of age, with good levels of milk production. They are maternal in nature, calm and easily handled. They have a long-life span and do well on the uplands, even in winter and do not need costly feed. As dual-purpose cattle, they have an average amount of muscle. Cows weigh about 550kg, whilst bulls weigh 750kg.

Meat

A steer, or castrated male is ready for killing after 30 months on the hills. He will produce fine-boned meat with a good killing out percentage, (which is the dead weight compared to his live weight), of greater than 60 per cent.

Milk

In an average lactation of 305 days, the cow will produce 3,500–6,000 litres on a forage-based diet. An outstanding cow could reach over 7,000 litres. The Northern Dairy Shorthorn cow can go on producing milk for 10 or more lactations. Protein levels in the milk are good at 3–3.25 per cent and buttermilk levels are also healthy, at 3.5–4.5 per cent.

Embryo Transfer

Due to the rarity of the Northern Dairy Shorthorn, embryos were taken to implant into surrogate mothers. This work has been carried out since 2015. Embryos are also preserved at the Rare Breeds Survival Trust Gene Bank.

The Northern Dairy Shorthorn is classified as Critical on the Rare Breeds Survival Trust's Watchlist, meaning that there are less than 150 breeding females.

VAYNOL

- The cows are very rare. Only four cows and two heifers made up the initial Scottish herd and there were originally only three cows in the Lincolnshire herd.
- The RBST have had success with artificial insemination, with the first calf born using this method in 2007. The semen was provided by a bull 30 years ago.

History

Vaynol cattle originally came from Scotland and are similar to the ancient British White Park cattle. In 1872 a herd was established at Vaynol Park in North Wales. The cattle were not domesticated, had little contact with humans and were considered to be wild. In 1980, the owner of the estate, Sir Michael Duff, died and the cattle were sold and moved to the Temple Newsam Estate near Leeds, which is owned by Leeds City Council.

In 2009, the group was split and three cows were taken to Lincolnshire to start a new herd. With the help of The Prince of Wales's Charitable Foundation a further starter herd was formed in Scotland. The variety of locations protects the cattle from disease, such as Foot and Mouth Disease.

Artificial Insemination

These cattle are very rare. Only four cows and two heifers (a cow that has not yet had a calf) made up the initial Scottish herd and there were originally only three cows in the Lincolnshire herd. The RBST have had success with artificial insemination, with the first calf born using this method in 2007. The semen was provided by a bull 30 years ago. With such a small population it is vital to reduce inbreeding and with that in mind, in 2006 the RBST set up a five-year genetic profiling programme.

RBST

Characteristics

Due to their semi-feral nature, these cattle are distrustful of humans. They are incredibly hardy and need very little care. They can tolerate all climates in the UK. They are a small to medium size cattle, with a primitive look – angular curving hocks and a sloping rump. They have slender, angular, medium-sized, upwardly-sweeping horns. Colours are white with black spots or totally black. Spots can cover the ears, eyelids, hooves, nose, point of the horns and socks. Females often have black teats on their udders. Milk yield tends to be poor. Bulls weigh between 400–450kg, whilst cows are 300–350kg.

Uses

Vaynol cattle are used for beef and producing leather. They are branded as upland beef. They are also exemplary conservation grazers due to their small size and frugal manner. They are happy to live on very poor grazing with very low nutritional requirements. In the past, they were considered wild, but due to human interaction resulting from their Critical status with the RBST, they have become semi-feral. They are still wary of humans, which is perhaps a good thing, given their horns. Due to their small size and weight they are less likely to harm delicate swards and weak soils.

Most cattle mature within 24-30 months on pasture, but the Vaynol takes its time. They are slow to mature and will not fully develop within this timescale unless given additional feed.

ENDANGERED (150 TO 250)

NATIVE ABERDEEN ANGUS

- The Native Aberdeen Angus should not be confused with the modern Aberdeen Angus, which is at the forefront of beef production. The modern Angus can reach a weight of 600kg in a year but will require roughly 4kg of daily concentrates in their feed in order to do so. The Native Angus will reach a similar weight by 18 months, feeding solely on grass and silage.
- As well as low input feeding, the Native Aberdeen Angus calves easily, with no intervention needed apart from winter feeding and artificial insemination.
- Black cattle have been recorded in Scotland since the sixteenth century. These were developed in the early nineteenth century using the slow developing, horned, black cattle of Forfarshire, which is today known as the county of Angus.
- The twentieth century saw large numbers of Native Aberdeen Anguses being exported to countries such as US, Canada, South America, Australia and New Zealand. Breeders in these counties tended to cross-breed further to create longer, bigger Anguses which were subsequently imported back into the UK, thereby jeopardising the breed standard in the original Angus population.

Native v Modern

The Native Aberdeen Angus should not be confused with the modern Aberdeen Angus, which is at the forefront of beef production. The modern Angus can reach a weight of 600kg in a year but will require roughly 4kg of daily concentrates in their feed in order to do so. The Native Angus will reach a similar weight by 18 months, feeding solely on grass and silage. The Native Angus delivers good quality meat living on poor grassland, which could be useful as modern developments such as housing and industry mean that less fertile land will have to be utilised. The modern Angus provides a bigger, faster-growing carcass with more sizable profits compared to the smaller native breed.

Native Benefits

As well as low input feeding, the Native Aberdeen Angus calves easily, with no intervention needed apart from winter feeding and artificial insemination.

RBST

They are docile and easy to look after, with cows producing calves at up to 12 or 14 years old. Native Aberdeen Angus calves are smaller than the modern Angus at birth, but still grow to be a good beef animal. Bulls are frequently crossed with dairy cows giving a more profitable beef calf. With a quiet temperament the Native Aberdeen Angus is a convenient solution for areas with public access.

Scottish Roots

Black cattle have been recorded in Scotland since the sixteenth century. These were developed in the early nineteenth century using the slow developing, horned, black cattle of Forfarshire, which is today known as the county of Angus. These cattle were hybridised with other breeds found in Aberdeenshire. Hugh Watson of Keillor Farm instigated the breed type and it was in 1824 that William McCombie, MP for South Aberdeenshire, made them well known. He did this incredibly well and the twentieth century saw large numbers of Native Aberdeen Anguses being exported to countries such as US, Canada, South America, Australia and New Zealand. Breeders in these counties tending to cross-breed further to create longer, bigger Anguses which were subsequently imported back into the UK, thereby jeopardising the breed standard in the original Angus population.

Black or Red?

The Native Aberdeen Angus is shorter in the leg than imported blood lines, and a lot stockier than the modern Angus. Animals are customarily black, but will occasionally be red. The udder can be white. They are polled, i.e. they have no horns, and cows will weigh in the region of 550kg, with bulls a little heavier, at 850kg. The Native Aberdeen Angus has no introduced genetics from either the modern breed or from abroad. The UK herd book registers both black and red animals, but in the US these have different herd books. The US had 324,266 registered black Anguses in 2005.

The first UK herd book was formed in 1862 and the breed society was created in 1879. The breed was well known throughout the UK by the mid-eighteenth century and was a mainstream breed in the mid-twentieth century.

Travels Abroad

The cattle first reached Argentina in 1879, when Don Carlos Guerrero bought in a bull and two cows. Aberdeen Anguses were first imported to Tasmania in the 1820s and reached the mainland in 1840. It grew in popularity, and is present in all Australian states and territories today, with a registered population of 62,000 calves in 2010. Canada saw its first Aberdeen Angus in 1876, when William Brown, a leading professor of agriculture, introduced a herd into the experimental farm at Ontario Agricultural College. In 1873, George Grant bought four Angus bulls to Victoria, Kanzas, with the American Angus Association established on 21 November 1883 in Chicago, Illinois. The Red Angus Association of America was created in 1954 as cattle were being removed from the herd book due to their colouration. The Germans hybridised their own breed of cattle; the German Angus, by cross-breeding the Angus with German Black Pied cattle, Gelbvieh and Fleckvieh, producing a larger specimen in black or red.

WHITEBRED SHORTHORN

Origins

The Whitebred Shorthorn, or White Shorthorn, is a breed of cattle that originally came from north-west England and south-west Scotland. 100 years ago, when it rose in prestige, it became known as the Cumberland White. It is a completely different breed from the Beef Shorthorn or Dairy Shorthorn which have been selectively bred for these aforementioned qualities. The Whitebred Shorthorn is always white, in comparison to the variety of colours shown by other Shorthorns.

Characteristics

The cattle are medium sized, weighing around 550–600kg for a female and 800–900kg for a male. In the past, their use was primarily as a beef cattle. Their outer coat is creamy white and they possess a chunky woollen undercoat. Cattle should have a wide muzzle, bold eyes and sound legs. Cows are excellent mothers, very docile, and able to give birth well into their teens. Whitebred Shorthorns are used for conservation grazing on hill pastures, as they help to create a wide variety of flora by removing invasive grass. They can withstand even the coldest of winters.

Adobe Stock

Crossing Sires

The other use that they have is as crossing sires. The Whitebred Shorthorn bull is used to breed with Galloway cows producing the esteemed Blue Grey. Other popular crosses are with the Highland, which creates a Cross Highlander. Both of these crosses breed hardy cattle, well suited to the extremes of British weather and able to do well even on the most inferior of land. The Blue Grey exhibits hybrid vigour, but it must breed throughout each generation using both varieties of parents as it does not breed true in the second generation.

Cattle Sales

It was in the late nineteenth century that Blue Grey cattle became popular. Mr David Hall of Larriston, Newcastleton, Roxburghshire and Mr Andrew Park of Stelshaw, Bailey, Cumberland put up for sale some Blue Grey suckled calves at the Newcastleton Suckler Sales. These calves were quick to mature into valuable beef cattle. The number of Whitebred Shorthorn been bred correspondingly increased, as the bulls were needed for cross-breeding, so much so, that at the turn of the twentieth century an individual day was needed at the Newcastleton Sales for these crosses.

Breed Association

Two hundred breeders gathered on 12 March 1962 to create the Whitebred Shorthorn Association, and breed society sales were conducted in the autumn of 1964 at Newcastleton and Bellingham. In 1965, a further sale was held in Newcastleton as well as in Botchergate Mart in Carlisle. The Breed Association continues to hold sales in Carlisle twice a year, in spring and autumn, however, these days the quantity of cattle sold is in single figures.

LINCOLN RED
(ORIGINAL POPULATION)

- Genetically, the Lincoln Red can trace their roots back to the wild Bos Urus cattle which came to Britain between 449 and 660AD, with Viking invaders from Scandinavia.
- In the 1700s and early 1800s, the Cherry-Red Durham and the York Shorthorn, some from the renowned herds of Robert Bakewell and the Collings brothers, were relocated to breed with the local Lincolnshire draught cattle to improve confirmation. The progeny were the Lincolnshire Red Shorthorn.
- Between 1904 and 1914, 744 Lincoln Reds were sent to 20 countries including the US, Argentina, Brazil, Australia, Canada, Germany, Hungary, New Zealand and South Africa. By 1926, the Lincoln Red Shorthorn was the second biggest breed of cattle being registered in England, after the Shorthorn (which had yet to be differentiated.)

Early Roots

The Lincoln Red cattle came from the county of Lincolnshire in the east of England. Genetically, they can trace their roots back to the wild Bos Urus cattle which came to Britain between 449 and 660AD, with Viking invaders from Scandinavia. Over 300 years ago Gervaise Markham wrote about the Lincolnshire cattle in his book, *A Way to get Wealth*.

Breed Development

In the 1700s and early 1800s, Britain was in a wave of breed development that swept the country. Both medium sized breeds, the Cherry-Red Durham and the York Shorthorn, some from the renowned herds of Robert Bakewell and the Collings brothers, were relocated to breed with the local Lincolnshire draught cattle to improve confirmation. The progeny were the Lincolnshire Red Shorthorn.

Herd Books

The cattle were described by the Board of Agriculture in 1799 as 'a breed of cattle which are unsurpassed in this country for points valuable and for

their disposition at any age to finish rapidly'. They were registered in the first volume of *Coates Herd Book* in 1822, but after the formation of The Lincoln Red Shorthorn Association in 1895, they began publishing their own herd book in 1896.

Exportation

Earliest recorded exports were in 1893, when Professor Wallace from Edinburgh University noted the beginning of The Argentine Red Lincolnshire Shorthorn Herd Book. Between 1904 and 1914, 744 Lincoln Reds were sent to 20 countries including the US, Argentina, Brazil, Australia, Canada, Germany, Hungary, New Zealand and South Africa.

Dual Purpose, Selectively Bred

By 1926, the Lincoln Red Shorthorn was the second biggest breed of cattle being registered in England, after the Shorthorn (which had yet to be differentiated into beef and dairy.) To start with, the Lincoln Red was a dual-purpose animal, but selective breeding resulted in separate beef and dairy breeds. Correspondingly, the herd book created two sections for the cattle, although beef production became more important and the final dairy registration was in 1965.

Creation of a Polled Cattle

In 1939, Eric Pentecost from Cropwell Butler, Nottinghamshire began selectively breeding the Lincoln Red Shorthorn to create polled cattle, using both black and red Aberdeen Angus bulls as crossing cattle. This work took 17 years, with the Lincoln keeping its original characteristics. The polled gene is valuable in that it saves time and money in not having to dehorn, and this trait is used commercially, with Lincoln Red bulls propagating this dominant gene. In 1960, the society removed the word 'Shorthorn' from its title and became the 'Lincoln Red Cattle Society'. No horned Lincoln Reds have been registered with the society since 1970.

Disastrous Importations

The 1970s and '80s saw importations of continental cattle breeds which initiated a decline in interest in indigenous British breeds. These European breeds were successfully crossed with Lincoln Reds to refine conformation and build up lean meat content. The traditional Lincoln Red was being lost, so much so, that it is now on the Rare Breeds Survival Trust Watchlist.

Characteristics of the Original Population

Lincoln Red cattle are long-lived, fertile and good mothers, producing calves up to 14 years of age, with milk yields reaching 3,600 litres per lactation, although they are now used for beef. They are docile animals, very easy to manage, and can cope with the coldest extremes of the British weather. Cows weigh in the region of 700–750kg, whilst bulls are 1,000–1,100kg. They exhibit a deep, cherry red colour, with no white allowed, apart from a small amount on the genitalia and tail brush. Their hair is short and fine in the summer, growing more dense and abundant in winter. They have a strong thick neck and a straight, muscled back with a well filled rump and skin that is silky to touch. They can be finished off with forage in 24–30 months or finished intensively at 12–14 months. They are robust and economical breed, useful for conservation grazing of any pasture.

At Risk (450 to 750)

Gloucester

> • In 1796, Sir Edward Jenner took the first anti-smallpox serum from a Gloucester cow named 'Blossom'. The word 'vaccination' comes from the Latin 'vacca', meaning 'cow'. Blossom's hide is still preserved by St George's Hospital in London.

Working hard in the Severn Valley

Cattle meeting the description of the Gloucester were found widely in the Cotswold Hills and Severn Valley from the thirteenth century. They were a tri-purpose breed, producing beef and milk, as well as being robust and placid draught oxen. Cheese was already being extensively made using their milk. By 1500, the settlement of Gloucester had gained a reputation for its successful cattle market and cheese and butter fair. The popularity of Gloucester cheese spread so that by the sixteenth to early eighteenth centuries it was even being exported to New England communities in America. At this time, herds of Gloucester cattle were found from Devon to Glamorgan and Essex.

Deadly Disease

Disaster struck from 1745–56 when the deadly rinderpest cattle disease arrived. This particular outbreak stood out with its intensity and duration. All cattle markets were stopped in Gloucester when outbreaks become common in 1748, with many farmers giving up cattle production and turning to arable instead. As the disease departed, Bakewell's improved Longhorn started to gain in strength and numbers, due to a greater profit margin from an enhanced quality of beef. This breed was in turn supplanted by the Shorthorn, bred by the Colling brothers, Charles and Robert, during the late eighteenth century.

Helping Medical Science

In 1796, Sir Edward Jenner took the first anti-smallpox serum from a Gloucester cow named 'Blossom'. The word 'vaccination' comes from the Latin 'vacca', meaning 'cow'. Blossom's hide is still preserved by St. George's Hospital in London.

Renewed Interest

A significant sale at Badminton in 1896 saw renewed interest in the breed, with the formation of the Gloucester Cattle Society in 1919. The first herd book listed 130 animals in 14 herds and totals rose considerably by 1925 to more than 300 bovines in 25 herds. However, foot and mouth was to strike, and by 1930 there were only 142 cattle in four herds.

Going, Going, Gone?

Badminton held the largest herd but disbanded it in 1950 as they had chronic infertility issues as a result of inbreeding. Colonel Elwes also dispersed his cattle that year, leaving a sum total of only 50 individuals in two herds. In 1965, the Hon. Ralph Bathurst died leaving his herd of 148 animals, and Eric Dowdeswell died in 1968, leaving his sisters to very sadly disperse the herd in 1972. However, enthusiasts were able to gather at the sale and bought each and every breeding female. In 1973, under the guidance of Charles Martell, the breed society revived and the herd book showed there were 70 cattle registered with 20 breeders. The breed is still 'At Risk' with fewer than 750 breeding females registered.

The 2001 Foot and Mouth epidemic could have been devastating to the Gloucesters, but luckily only a few were lost.

Strikingly Beautiful

Gloucesters are known to be a joy to keep, with a placid, easy going nature.

They calve well, usually with no intervention needed, and calves are generally robust and healthy. They are of medium size, long in the body, with cows weighing 500–600kg and bulls 750–850kg. They are beautiful animals, with a rich dark brown body and a black head and legs. They possess a white stripe that flows down their backs, covering the tail, and over the udders and underbelly. They are of medium length, with upwardly sweeping, white horns tipped in black.

Delicious Cheeses

Gloucester cows average about 3,700 litres every lactation, although some cows produce 5,000 litres. They have a flat lactation curve, meaning that they give an even rate of production lasting up to 300 days. They can give birth up to the age of 12–15 years. They are ideal house cows as they are happy to hand milk. Their milk tends to have a butterfat content of 3.9 per cent, protein of 3.3 per cent and lactose of 4.6 per cent. The small fat globules and high protein content mean that it is perfect for making cheese. Single Gloucester and Stinking Bishop cheeses must be created specifically from milk from Gloucester cows. Double Gloucester cheese, once typically made from Gloucester milk, can now be made from any cow's milk. Gloucester beef has seen an upward trend of popularity.

BRITISH WHITE

- British White cattle are white with black or red points on the ears, muzzle, hooves, fetlocks and teats.
- Black points carry the dominant gene with red occurring in only two per cent of cattle.
- They were used commercially for milk production in the UK until the 1960s. Beef production is also popular.
- They look very similar to White Park cattle, although they do not have horns and are slightly stockier.
- British White have a dark skin pigmentation which means they can tolerate heat – making them popular in Australia and the Midwest US.
- In 1918, at the formation of the Park Cattle Society in the UK, there were only seven herds, with 16 bulls and 115 females.

Monastic Roots

The British White dates back to the seventeenth century, when Richard Assheton acquired Whalley Abbey in Lancashire after the dissolution of the monasteries. In 1765, Mary Assheton married Lord Suffield who lived in Gunton Hall in Norfolk. In doing so, she took with her a few of the white polled cattle from Whalley.

East Anglian Heritage

East Anglia became the significant focus for the British White with the Gunton herd going on to form two major herds. One began in the years 1793 to 1812 when Lord Suffield's daughter-in-law, Lady Caroline Harbord, took some British White to Blickling near Aylsham in Norfolk when she inherited the place. There was a lethal cattle plague around 1860, which left only two creatures alive, but care and time saw a renaissance in this herd.

Dominant Black Points

The second foundation herd from Gunton was created at Woodbastwick in 1840 from the sale of a selection of British Whites by the forth Lord Suffield. The breeders at Woodbastwick preferred British Whites with red points, and

British White Cattle Societ

would transfer all black pointed animals to Blickling. However, the majority of cattle, (around 98 per cent), were black pointed, as this is the dominant gene.

Foundation Herds

There was a herd at Somerford Park, Cheshire, kept by Sir Walter Shakerley, but no records of the breed history of this herd exist. The Northrepps herd was created in 1890, using a bull from Woodbastwick and a cow from Blickling. The transfer of bulls between this herd and the Woodbastwick and Shakerley stock in the years up to 1918 successfully combined the gene pool of all these foundation herds.

Cattle Societies

By the inception of the Park Cattle Society in 1918 three other herds were considered important. The largest of these was at Bawdeswell, which had sprung from the Northrepps herd, which was apportioned by the Gurney family in 1912. Another was the Kelmarsh herd, which originated in 1903 using British Whites from the Blickling herd. The third was the Faygate herd which came about in 1908 and was made up of horned and polled animals. It was not until 1918 that they were segregated into two divisions, determined by whether they had horns or not. By 1946 the two different branches of the Society made the decision to separate, and the British White Cattle Society of today was formed for the polled bovines.

Heat Tolerant Animals

British White cattle have no horns, and are of medium size, with cows weighing 550–700kg and bulls, 900–1100kg. They are usually white with black, (sometimes red), points on the ears, muzzle, hooves, fetlocks and teats. They have a dark skin pigmentation, meaning that they can tolerate the heat well, making them useful animals in Australia and the Midwest US.

Dual Purpose

British White cows were used for commercial milk production in the UK up to the 1960s, with yields of 5,000 litres not being uncommon. They are dual purpose, with beef production also being popular. Without horns, they are easy to manage and cows calve easily and are good mothers, producing young into their teens. They are thrifty grazers, surviving on rough pastures eating rushes, heathers and nettles, and can outwinter in most climates. They are very similar in looks to the White Park cattle, having the same red or black points with a white coat. However, the White Park has horns, which are white with black tips. The British White is stockier with slightly more spotting and darker points.

Survival

In 1918, at the creation of the Park Cattle Society, there were only seven herds with 16 bulls and 115 females. By 1990, with increased awareness of the British White, there were 116 herds with more than 1,500 registered cattle. The RBST allocates them a 'Minority' status which means that there are between 750 and 1,500 registered breeding females today. In 2019, a herd of 45 British White cattle were introduced to clear invasive bracken in Blenheim Estate's ancient woodland in Oxfordshire.

Grading Up Register to Keep the Breed Alive

In the past, such was the struggle to keep the breed going, occasionally other breeds were incorporated, so as to avoid inbreeding, whilst still creating the preferred type. The Park Cattle Society, in 1928, started a grading up register, permitting breeders to register half bred cattle which would be qualified for pedigree status at the fifth cross with pedigree blood. The British White Cattle Society decided to bring closure to this system in 1996, which is a testament to the strength of numbers of the cattle which they are trying to protect.

British White Cattle Societies Overseas

The British White Cattle Society of Australia published its first herd book in 1985. North America has two societies; the British White Cattle Association of America and the American British White Park Association – although this is concerned with the British White not the White Park!

IRISH MOILED

- Skeletal remains dating back to 640AD show the presence of hornless bovines in Ireland, with written legends of 'red, white backed cattle'.
- Viking raids in 1000AD are evident by the East Finn polled cattle, with parallel colouring, found in Scandinavia today.
- The Irish Moiled produces delicious tender meat with a very distinct flavour.

Viking Raids

The term 'Moile' or 'Moal' in Gaelic means 'bald', referring to the polled head of these cattle. It also references their distinctive mound-shaped head.

These cattle originate from County Leitrim, Country Sligo, County Down and County Donegal in Ireland. Skeletal remains dating back to 640AD show the presence of hornless bovines in Ireland, (predating the Norse and Danish invasions), with written legends of 'red, white backed cattle'. Viking raids in 1000AD are evident by the East Finn polled cattle with parallel colouring found in Scandinavia today.

Best Cow in Ulster!

Once commonplace in the nineteenth century throughout Ireland, the breed declined due to beef and dairy specialisation. The breed society was started in 1926 with the aim of developing a dual-purpose animal that could be kept on any ground. A cow called 'Greyabbey Kate' won the Caldwell Cup for being the best cow in Ulster, due to her extremely high milk yields, not to mention producing 16 calves in the 22 years that she lived. The war interrupted the work of the society but in 1948 it was revived again by Mr A.E.H. Gillespie, whereby a bull named 'Hakku' was bought over from Finland to restore fortunes.

Red Tape, Epidemics and Genetic Research

The Agricultural Act Northern Ireland 1949 expressed that only cows that had registered a high milk yield could have their male offspring licenced.

This was problematic as the majority of owners worked on a small scale, not chronicling individual milk production, and subsequently there were very few bulls to keep the breed alive. By October 1982, Belfast Zoo, the National Trust and the RBST worked with a handful of committed farmers with 20 cows and two bulls remaining. The BSE epidemic in 1996 closed trading of live animals between EU countries until 2006. The Irish attempted to increase numbers of the Irish Moiled with little success throughout this time, although the Republic of Ireland and Northern Irish governments did receive an EU subsidy as the status of the cattle as a rare native breed was recognised. By 2010, the Irish Moiled cattle were back on track. Genetic research at Liverpool University throughout the 1980s and '90s by Dr Ian Gill had paid off and Liverpool City Council and Leeds City Council purchased several of the breed. The cattle were shown at the Royal Ulster Agricultural Show in 2013, for the first time in 80 years.

Beautiful Colouring and Docile Temperaments

The cattle are remarkably docile and very easy to manage. This easy-going nature made them perfect for ploughing in days gone by. They produce delicious tender meat with a very distinct flavour and can finish on a forage-based system in 20–24 months with a deadweight of 220–260kg. They originated from coarse and exposed land and can survive on land that is difficult for other cattle, such as marshy situations. They are ideal conservation grazers, eating a variety of food such as willow, ash and ivy. They do need extra hay in serious climatic conditions but will grow a thick winter coat. Cows produce yields of 4,500–6,500 litres even on poor ground. This milk has a butterfat content of over 4 per cent and a protein level of 3.3 per cent. Cows weigh on average 600kg, with steers (young bulls) at 800kg. The animal has beautiful markings with a red or roan body and a white line, known as 'finching', running along the back and tail, reaching under to the teats and underbelly. The nose and ears are red, with the face frequently speckled. White will appear in varying quantities on the body.

SHETLAND

- There are two theories for the origins of Shetland cattle: one is that Neolithic people captured wild aurochs in 3000BC. The other is that they came over with the Norse invaders in 1000AD.
- They were aligned closely with the crofting lifestyle found in the Shetlands.
- After the Second World War, the government withdrew subsidies for the cattle, unless they were cross-bred with larger beef breeds. By the 1950s, there were fewer than 40 pure bred cattle left.

Neolithic or Norse?

There are two theories for the origins of Shetland cattle; one is that Neolithic people captured the wild aurochs in 3000BC that ranged the woodlands of Britain and Europe following the last Ice Age. Archaeological evidence in Shetland and Orkney supports this. The other idea is that they came over with the Norse invaders in 1000AD, since the Shetland is very similar to the South and Westland cattle found scarcely in south-western Norway today.

High Butterfat Content for the Children

Whatever their origin, they were aligned closely with the crofting lifestyle found in the Shetlands, particularly subsistence farming, where their milking qualities in particular were highly valued for nutrition for the children while the men were away at sea, trying to eke a living. An average lactation is rather low, at 2,500 litres, but the milk has a high butterfat content. At the beginning of the 1800s there were thought to be 15,000 Shetland cattle on the island. As transport and the economy of the island improved in the mid-1800s, the

government asked islanders to cross-breed their Shetlands with larger beef breeds. This was successful, as the Shetland cow has enough milk to rear a larger cross, and with a wide pelvis, the cows are able to calve easily.

Only 40 left...

After the Second World War, the government withdrew subsidies unless the Islanders cross-bred their Shetland cattle again with the larger beef breeds. Purebred Shetlands became increasingly scarce and they only regained their status when they were classified as a dual-purpose breed in the 1950s. At that time, there were fewer than 40 purebred cattle left. Shetland cattle have gathered a lot of support over the years, much of it coming from mainland UK. There are presently 800 breeding females with 180 calves registered annually. Apart from cross-breeding, it is used for conservation grazing and smallholders enjoy it for its tame and sweet temperament. Its meat is excellent

Mary K

and it sells for high prices through the Traditional Breeds Meat Marketing Scheme. It can be slaughtered within 30 months off poor grazing.

Viking horns!

The cows weigh 350–450kg, with the bulls weighing 550–600kg. They are usually black, or black and white. Around 10 per cent are red and white, but they are also seen in red, dun, grey, brown and brindle (streaked). They exhibit small, curving, 'Viking' horns.

TRADITIONAL HEREFORD

- The Traditional Hereford originally came from the Welsh Marshes around the Black and Cambrian Mountains in Wales.
- Export of the Hereford began in 1817, with more than five million Herefords now present in more than 50 countries.

Origins in the Marshes

The Traditional Hereford originally came from the Welsh Marshes around the Black and Cambrian Mountains in Wales, following the flow of the rivers that took them into Herefordshire, Shropshire and Worcestershire. They were able to utilise this environment, preferentially eating rough vegetation, including a number of trees and shrubs to become the low input, early maturing cattle that we know today.

Strict Entry Requirements

Originally, these beasts were made to work with the plough for five to six years, before being sent to market. However, the first herd book was established in 1846, with the Hereford Cattle Society formed in 1878, patronised by Queen Victoria. Since 1886, no cattle are allowed in the herd book, unless both the sire and dam have already been entered.

Mass Exodus

Export of the Hereford began in 1817, with more than five million Herefords now present in more than 50 countries, including the US, Canada, Mexico, Israel, Japan, Europe, Scandinavia and of course, the famous cattle lands of South America. In 1951 a World Hereford Council was created, drawing together all the different Hereford Cattle Societies in so many countries.

Herouldmede Traditional Heref

Muddying the Gene Pool

In the 1960s and '70s some UK breeders looked to US bloodlines with the aim of lengthening the legs of their Traditional Herefords. They were also hoping for an animal that could compete with the popular continental breeds. However, by 1995, breeders were getting concerned with the dilution of genes in their stock and so added the suffix * to any cattle that remained true to the British Hereford herd book.

High Maintenance

Agriculture was changing and the focus moved to high input and high output farming, using cereal based diets to create a larger framed animal. The bigger, slow maturing cattle developed in Canada and the US ousted the Hereford, which was low input, early maturing. But in the Traditional Hereford's favour, things have come full circle and their ability to convert a low quality pasture to quality meat has secured their popularity over recent years, with numbers growing to reflect that.

Signature White Face

The signature of the Traditional Hereford is its white face. Even cross-bred calves will share this feature. They are of medium size, with cows weighing 450–550kg and bulls 750–850kg. They are red, with a white stripe along the length of the body going into the underbelly. The animals are horned, but these are often detached. A cow will calve up to 14 years old, useful for suckling calves for beef or for dairy operations.

WHITE PARK

- The White Park is believed to be the oldest breed of cattle in Britain.
- Early mentions of the White Park Cattle go back over 2,000 years to pre-Christian Irish legends.
- World War Two saw the Government ship a handful of these creatures to the US for safe keeping as they were a valued part of British heritage.
- Only 60 cattle still survived by the time the RBST formed in 1973.

2,000 Year History

Early mentions of the White Park Cattle go back over 2,000 years to pre-Christian Irish legends, for example, 'Tain Bo Cualgnel' or 'The Cattle Raid of Cooley'. Other records show the Laws of Hywel Dda in Wales, where punishments were paid in cattle. Dynevor Castle in Wales was an important political and military stronghold and again, in the Dimetian Code of Laws, cattle were a powerful bargaining point. The White Park is believed to be the oldest breed of cattle in Britain.

The advent of Roman rule pushed the Druids and these cattle to the north and west of the UK and into Ireland, and the ancient herds of pre-1500AD were formed. The Dynevor and Cadzow herds are still thriving today. The Chartley and Drumlanrig herds, both with ancient roots, were disbanded in 1905 and 1780, although they have been regenerated latterly.

Middle Ages Manoeuvres

Most native breeds cannot trace their roots by more than 200–300 years, but the White Park go back thousands of years. In ancient texts they are occasionally mentioned as 'White Forest' cattle, due to their native woodland habitat. They have direct links to the wild cattle that roamed the UK in ancient times but were enclosed by nobility in parkland throughout the Middle Ages, starting with Henry III's jurisdiction in 1225. However, by the turn of the twentieth century these parks fell in popularity, and cattle numbers subsequently declined. Of the 12 or so herds that existed in the early nineteenth century, most were slaughtered.

Wales was the first place where White Park cattle were recorded. Comparable to earlier Irish practices, the Laws of Hywel Dda calculated fines and remuneration as payable by white cattle with coloured points. The Dimetian Code of Laws also stated that fines must be settled with the Lord of Dynevor by handing over a certain number of the cattle. Dynevor Castle was

Laura Corbett

an important area in Welsh history for over 500 years, with the Prince of South Wales using Dynenor Castle as his stronghold from 800AD. One recorded incident shows the spouse of William de Breos (Brecon), trying to give King John a White Park bull and 400 cows in 1210AD in an attempt to placate him, which apparently did not work!

World War Two saw the Government ship a handful of these creatures to the US for safe keeping as they were a valued part of British heritage. By the 1960s, just four herds remained – Dynevor, Cadzow, Woburn and Whipsnade, with only 60 cattle still surviving by the time the RBST formed in 1973. The Trust chose the White Park cattle for its logo.

Semi-Feral Relatives

The Chillingham Wild Cattle in Northumberland and the Vaynol Cattle of Wales are both semi-feral breeds. The Chillingham Wild Cattle are thought to have diverged from the White Park cattle many years ago.

In the US the cattle are called Ancient White Park, as the British White cattle are known in the US as the American White Park.

Porcelain White with Black Points

The White Park is a medium to large beast, with bulls weighing 800–1,000kg and cows, 500–700kg. They are a beautiful porcelain white, with black (occasionally red) points – muzzle, ears, eye rims, feet, teats and horn tips. They have long horns, which in cows have an elegant forwards and upwards curve. The bulls' horns are stockier and stubbier. White Parks thrive on a non-intensive system and are most at home on coarse ground. In the past they were triple purpose, pulling a plough as well as for meat and milk. Nowadays, meat is the speciality, commanding high prices and an enviable reputation.

EQUINE

CRITICAL
(FEWER THAN 300 BREEDING FEMALES)

Cleveland Bay Horse
Dales Pony
Eriskay Pony
Hackney Horse and Pony
Suffolk Horse

ENDANGERED
(300 TO 500)

Dartmoor Pony
Exmoor Pony

VULNERABLE
(500 TO 900)

Clydesdale Horse
Fell Pony
Highland Pony

AT RISK
(900 TO 1500)

New Forest Pony
Shire Horse

CRITICAL
(FEWER THAN 300 BREEDING FEMALES)

CLEVELAND BAY HORSE

- Many Cleveland Bays were active in the First World War, being used as artillery horses.
- After the Second World War, in 1945, the breed was in grave danger of being lost forever.
- Queen Elizabeth II came to the rescue. She bought the stallion, Mulgrave Supreme. In the following 15 years, 36 purebred stallions were born in Britain.
- A 2006 survey showed that there are 550 purebred Cleveland Bays in the world.
- The Equus Survival Trust estimates 100–300 breeding females internationally.

History

The Cleveland Bay dates back to before records were kept. They were originally bred in the Middle Ages in the Cleveland Hills in Yorkshire. They were kept by the clergy to use as pack horses carrying supplies between monasteries and abbeys in the north-east of England, as well as by merchants who needed to take wool from farms to mills. In the seventeenth century they were known as 'Chapman Horses', since they were put to use to pull the heavy carts used by travelling tradesmen called 'Chapmen'.

Carriages

The first carriages were invented during the reign of Queen Elizabeth I, but it was not until the late eighteenth century that roads improved and the purpose of the Cleveland Bay changed. Rather than needing it for strength and perseverance, it was cross-bred with Andalusian and Barb horses and latterly Thoroughbreds and Arabians to produce the Cleveland Bay that we know today. These horses were developed to have a lighter frame, a well-arched neck, and muscular shoulders well suited for pulling carriages.

Exportation and Artillery Work

With the invention of the railways, the horses fell out of favour and by the 1880s the breed was in danger of extinction. Many Cleveland Bays had been

exported overseas: to New Zealand, Australia, the United States and South Africa. The Cleveland Bay Horse Society, in Britain, was formed in 1883, opening its stud book in 1884. The Cleveland Bay Horse Society of America started in 1885. Many horses were active in the First World War, being used as artillery horses. After the Second World War, in 1945, the breed was in grave danger of being lost forever.

Royal Rescue

Queen Elizabeth II came to the rescue. She bought the stallion, Mulgrave Supreme, who was meant for export, and made him available for stud. In the following 15 years, 36 purebred stallions were born in Britain. Prince Phillip, the Duke of Edinburgh used Cleveland Bays in international driving competitions. The breed is successful in all spheres, most obviously in driving and dressage and in show-jumping, producing Olympic performances. Today, Cleveland Bays and Thoroughbred crosses are used to pull the royal carriages.

The horse is suitable as a hunter and can carry a 110kg man all day, over heavy ground and with big jumps.

In Danger of Extinction

Despite the surge in popularity since the 1970s, a 2006 survey revealed that there are in the region of 550 purebred Cleveland Bays in the world today. This is a serious figure. The Equus Survival Trust estimates that there are between 100–300 breeding females in the world. The RBST reports that 64 of these mares are in the United Kingdom.

Cross-Breeding

The Cleveland Bay's attributes, such as endurance, muscularity and jumping ability were used extensively in the 1860s to create other breeds, such as the Oldenburg breed. Other breeds that have benefited are the Holstein and Hanoverian. Many European Warmblood horses have a Cleveland Bay descent. They are also used to lighten draught horse breeds. Cleveland Bays are particularly popular when crossed with Thoroughbreds. It is the chestnut Thoroughbred ancestry that sometimes causes a Cleveland Bay to have red legs, rather than the desired black.

Characteristics

The horse stands between 16 and 16.2 hands (163–168cm). They are bay in colour with no white markings, apart from the occasional small star. On occasion, there will be some grey hairs present in the mane and tail. This is a feature of some pure bloodlines. Cleveland Bay horses will have black points, with totally black lower legs.

The horse has a broad chest, with a short back and sloping shoulders that are deep and strong. The head is large, with kind eyes and large ears. The legs are unfeathered, as historically they were used to work in heavy soils, and feathered legs attracted disease. They have a calm temperament and are hardy and long-lived. It is important that their feet are blue and strong. They must not be too narrow or shallow.

DALES PONY

- The 1700s brought a great improvement in the roads, and hence the arrival of the mail and stagecoach, which needed quick ponies to pull them. The fast Norfolk Cobs were bred into the Dales pony bloodlines.
- The Dales ponies served in both World Wars.
- After the Second World War, numbers were so low that the pony nearly disappeared altogether.
- In 1955 only four new fillies were recorded.
- A white star or snip is allowed on the head, according to the Breed Standard, but not stripes, blazes or white muzzles.

Ancient history

Horses have been in the Dales area for centuries. Horse bones from the Roman era have been discovered around Ribcester. The Romans tell of an ancient British people living in the east of the Pennines, who they called the Gabrantovici, or 'horse-riding warriors'.

Dales Pony Society

Indigenous roots

The ponies are indigenous to the eastern slopes of the Pennines, ranging from High Peak in Derbyshire to the Cheviot Hills near the Scottish border. Breeding grounds have always been found in the higher dales of the Tyne, Wear, Tees, Swale and Allen rivers.

Roman mining

Since Roman times they have been used in the lead mining industry. This industry was highly dependent on geography. The high moors held the rakes of lead. Washing needed to be done in a stream and smelting required wood and a windy hillside. The native ponies were perfect for carrying the iron ore, fuel for smelting and the finished lead. They worked in teams of between 9–20 ponies, loose-headed (i.e. not led), whilst supervised by a single mounted man.

The Scotch Galloway

In the late 1600's it was decided to mix other breeds in with the Dales pony. The Scotch Galloway was chosen because they had particularly deep and clean legs, aiding their speed and robustness over difficult terrain. The Dales pony already had a reputation for their enormous strength and endurance over rugged country. Dales pony mares ran with the Scotch stallions and produced a pony that could carry a pack load of 109kg, (which was known as two pigs of lead), and travel 100 miles every week over complex and extreme terrain.

Farming work

Farmers also made use of these qualities and the fact that the ponies could cope with the acute weather on the Dales. They took the ponies to use for draught and other farm work. They could pull a ton of weight when pulling a cart, and could aid shepherds, carrying up to 76kg of hay and a rider, traversing appreciable distances in heavy snow. The ponies were highly valued on the farm but with the advent of steam, generally numbers fell. Many ponies found work in the north-east, in coal and lead mines.

Improvement in the 1700s

Improvements in the roads in the late 1700s brought a great improvement in the roads, and hence the arrival of the mail and stagecoach, which needed quick ponies to pull them. The speedy Norfolk Cobs, principally the Shales, were bred into the Dales pony bloodlines. One Shale in particular, was Shales the Original, foaled in 1755 and fathered by Blaze, who was himself sired by Flying Childers, who was by Darley Arabian. Darley Arabian was highly influential, being the foundation stallion that sired most of the world's quality trotting breeds today.

Dales Pony Improvement Society protecting bloodlines

Trotting races, held in the eighteenth century bought much success to the Dales ponies. In the nineteenth century the Welsh Cob, Comet was introduced into the bloodline to increase the height of the Dales ponies. Some Fell pony blood was also added to the existing bloodline, but in 1916 the Dales Pony Improvement Society was formed, after Clydesdale blood looked like it was going to ruin the original Dales pony breed. These Clydesdales were used to create 'vanners' and 'gunners'; for town work and the army respectively. The Dales Pony stud book was organised, to secure the conservation of the breed.

Army work

In the early 1920s, 200 Dales ponies were bought by the British Army. They were very specific about their requirements: ponies had to be older than five years, 14.0–14.2 hands (142.2–146.2cm) high at the withers, weigh more than 450kg, girth of 170cm and were able to carry more than 133kg over mountains.

Dedicating breeding

The Dales pony served in both World Wars. After the Second World War, numbers were so low that it nearly disappeared altogether. In 1955 only four new fillies were recorded. A handful of very dedicated breeders restructured the Dales Pony Society in 1964, dropping the word 'Improvement'. A 'Grading-Up' system was introduced, intended to identify and breed ponies with original Dales qualities. This programme was so successful that it closed in 1971 having achieved its aims. Enough ponies had been bred to allow breeders to export – 12 to Canada in 1991 and 4 to the US in 1994. By the turn of the millennium in 1999, 60 ponies were registered in North America, with 800 worldwide. 1999 also saw the creation of the Dales Pony Society of America as a sub-registry of the British Society.

Characteristics

The Dales pony is put together well, with a short back, muscular loins and strong, powerful legs and quarters. They have pony ears, which are slightly incurving. Their withers are not too narrow. The Breed Standard states that they should stand between 14.0–14.2 hands (142.2–146.2cm). Typically, they will be black, but other colours are brown, bay, roan and very seldom, grey. The head carriage is high, and they possess a long, flowing mane and tail, with plenty of sleek feathers on their heels. A white star or snip is allowed on the head, according to the Breed Standard, but not stripes, blazes or white muzzles. White fetlocks on the hind legs are allowed. If they do not meet the required standard they are listed in the B register in the stud book.

Uses

Their fast, stylish trot coupled with their calm nature makes the Dales pony a sought after driving and dressage pony. They are a popular choice when it comes to riding, due to their good conformation, vitality and calibre. They also possess enormous stamina, which makes them ideal for long-distance riding and trekking. They are willing and agile jumpers, capable in the fields of show-jumping, cross-country and eventing. Their great strength makes them useful for forestry work.

Health

The Dales pony, as well as the Fell pony both carry the fatal genetic disorder foal immunodeficiency syndrome (FIS). This is a recessive gene, which will only affect a foal if both parents are carriers. A study in 2010 found that 12 per cent of Dales Ponies are carriers. Genetic testing allows breeders to choose wisely when using a sire. The disease occurs after birth. Death will happen before three months as the pony will suffer from anaemia, and with an immune system that does not properly function, the condition becomes fatal.

Today

Today, the Dales pony is listed as 'Criticial' with the Rare Breeds Survival Trust, meaning that there are fewer than 300 breeding females registered in the UK today. There are small feral herds in the eastern Pennines. 2007 estimates these herds accounted for 30 mares who are of the age to breed.

ERISKAY PONY

- A few original Eriskay ponies are still on the island of Eriskay and they have not undergone cross-breeding.
- From a population of 20 in the 1970s, things have got better for the Eriskay pony, although the RBST still classifies them as Critical.
- By 2009, there were thought to be 420 Eriskay ponies in the world.
- There is a small herd of wild Eriskay ponies on Holy Island off the coast of Northumberland.

Ancient roots

The Eriskay pony evolved in the Hebrides, a group of islands to the west of Scotland. The breed is ancient, with roots in Celtic and Norse equines and is physically very similiar to the depictions of ponies on Pictish stones present throughout the North and West of Scotland. It also has roots in breeds living in the north, such as the Faroe pony and Icelandic horse. The island of Eriskay, in the Outer Hebrides, lends its name to the pony.

Donald McGillivray

Crofter's work

The Eriskay pony was once numerous across the islands. Up until the mid-nineteenth century 'Western Isles type' ponies were used widely as crofter's ponies, working on common tasks such as bringing home peat to burn to warm the home in winter, and seaweed to nourish the land that they lived off. They did this with the use of panniers made from basket work, which was slung over their backs. They would help to plough the land, draw carts and take the children to school.

Cross-breeding and Mechanisation

The nineteenth century saw the increase in cross-breeding to produce larger animals for farm work and transportation. Horses, such as Arabs and Clydesdales and the Norwegian Fjord were used to improve native Scottish ponies. However, the ponies on the remote island of Eriskay did not undergo cross-breeding. Because of the mechanisation of farming, the stock had become low – that of 20 ponies by the early 1970s.

Unusual fact

One usual fact about the Eriskay pony – the SS *Politician* got into trouble just off the Eriskay coast in 1941. The people of the island, with the help of the Eriskay ponies, assisted the removal of their cargo – some 250,000 bottles of whiskey!

Characteristics

The pony stands 12.0–13.2 hands (124–138cm) high and is generally grey in colour. Foals are born either black or bay, and the majority of them mature to be grey. A few, however, retain their young colouration. These darker animals should possess a light-coloured muzzle and have a light ring circling the eye. A pronounced dorsal stripe (which is a primitive marking) should not be present. They have a thick waterproof coat in winter, adapted to the harsh environment in which they live. This turns to a fine, glossy coat in the summer. Their mane and tail are not overly coarse. They share a lot of physical traits with the Exmoor pony.

They have short, high steps which run smoothly without overemphasis. With an active, honest manner they are exceptionally good with humans. This is due to years of working with humans as a croft pony, where they would be part of family life.

Breed Standard

The Breed Standard, also called a bench standard or standard of point, is an established set of guidelines which make sure that the breeder produces

animals that satisfy the requirements of a standardised breed. Chestnut, piebald and skewbald ponies, as well as those with excessive white markings are not generally accepted by the breed standard.

Breed societies

Two breed societies exist for the Eriskay pony. In 1971, the Eriskay Pony (Purebred) Studbook Society or Comann Each nan Eilean was founded, followed by the Eriskay Pony Society in 1986. The former forbids cross-breeding and wants to keep the breed pure, whilst the later considers cross-breeding as a useful function, to produce quality ponies and thereby ensure the survival of the breed.

Conservation Grazing

The breed is extremely hardy and has a thrifty nature which makes them excellent at conservation grazing.

Riding

Eriskay ponies are small, strong and well suited to driving, where they have been successful at international level competitions. They have an exceptionally friendly nature which means they are ideal for working with the disabled and special needs children. They can also be used for three-day eventing, show jumping, dressage, hunting, show hunter, pony club eventing, team games, western riding and light draught work. Their affectionate nature makes them a perfect family pony.

Today

From a population of 20 in the 1970s, things have got better for the Eriskay pony, although the RBST still classifies them as Critical, with fewer than 300 breeding females in the UK. Numbers in 2006 stated that there were approximately 300 mares and four purebred stallions globally. By 2009, there were thought to be 420 Eriskay ponies in the world.

An additional pure bred, wild population

There is a small herd of wild Eriskay ponies on Holy Island off the coast of Northumberland. Originally five ponies were brought to the island, in the 1970s, to create a nature reserve by the then owners, Universities Federation for Animal Welfare. The island has since changed hands, to the Samye Buddhist Centre for World Peace and Health, and the ponies continue to live happily there.

HACKNEY HORSE AND PONY

- In 1800, a Hackney mare, Phenomenon, was raced for 17 miles, at a trot, to see if she could do it within 56 minutes. There was a £400 bet on her! She did it in 53 minutes.
- Stud book records go back to 1755.
- The Hackney pony was evolved by Christopher Wilson using Sir George, a Hackney stallion foaled in 1866 to breed with Fell Pony mares.
- Hackney horses and ponies frequently show white markings, due to the sabino gene, of which little is understood
- They are known as the 'ballerinas of the show ring' with their magnificent high-stepping trot.

History

In the fourteenth century, the King of England demanded to have horses that were elegant but strong. Hackney horses were the breed he chose to develop. Later on, down the line, in 1542, the then King of England, King Henry VIII needed exceptionally forward-going horses to use in war. He decreed that each wealthy subject keep a certain number of Hackney horses to breed for this purpose.

The sixteenth and seventeenth centuries saw an improvement in the roads. Carriage driving became more popular, and it was the height of fashion to be seen out in an elegant equipage with these stylish, high-stepping equines.

The Modern Hackney

Although the British Hackney horse has been recorded since medieval times, it was developed with Norfolk and Yorkshire Roadsters, (trotting horses), during the eighteenth and nineteenth centuries, starting in 1729, with a Norfolk Trotter stallion and an Arabian stallion contributing their genes. The result was called a Norfolk Roadster and was powerfully built and useful for farm work.

Darley Arabian was an amazing horse, being one of three stallions that created the thoroughbred breed. He too had influence on the Norfolk Trotter, by his grandson, the undefeated racehorse, Flying Childers, whose son, the stallion Blaze, foaled Original Shales in 1755. This horse then went on to produce two stallions, Scot Shales and Driver, who both had enormous impact on the Norfolk Trotter breed.

Endurance Trotting Races

These horses had immense stamina and elegance. They were bred with Yorkshire trotting mares for their high-stepping trot which they could maintain for prolonged periods. Phenomenon, the Hackney mare was raced against the clock – she had to trot 17 miles in 56 minutes with a bet of £400 over her. In 1800 this was a lot of money! Needless to say, she did it in 53 minutes, a pace which her daughter managed to equal, two years later at only 14 hands (142.2cm) high.

Norfolk and Yorkshire Trotter

The Norfolk and Yorkshire Trotter were selectively bred for speed and elegance and created the foundations of the modern Hackney horse. With the onset of motorisation in the early twentieth century the need for this breed declined. However, the grace and style of the breed managed to pull it through and it found its niche in the show ring.

Stud Book

The Hackney Horse Society was created in Norwich in 1883, with stud book records going back to 1755. The breed was very popular overseas and has had some impact on the Continental Warmbloods, notably Holsteins and Gelderlanders. The pony element of the Hackney breed is incorporated in this stud book. The word, Hackney, comes from the French, 'haquenée' which translates as 'riding horse'. Hackneys have also been exported to the United States and Australia.

Pony

The Hackney breed is one of a very few breeds that have both horse and pony elements. The ponies have their roots as carriage ponies, but today they are foremost used as show ponies.

Breed Development

The pony was evolved by Christopher Wilson using Sir George, a Hackney stallion, born in 1866, coupling with Fell Pony mares using the progeny to create a new breed. He wanted the pony version of the horse with the emphasised trot and speed.

These creations were called Wilson ponies. They were left out all year, in the harsh Fell weather with little food or warmth. By the 1880s, Wilson was satisfied. He had created a new breed which incorporated the style and trotting aptitude of the Hackney horse. These ponies were used extensively as carriage ponies and found great popularity in the US. As with the horse, the rise of the car meant the demise of the carriage, and by the end of the Second World War these ponies were in serious decline. They found popularity in the show ring, which ultimately saved them.

Characteristics

Horse

A Hackney horse stands 14.2 hands (147cm) to 16.2 hands (168cm) high. They are characteristically bay or black but can be brown or chestnut. They frequently show white markings, which are due to the sabino gene or gene complex of which little is understood. Therefore, breeding specifically for these white markings can be unpredictable.

The Hackney horse has a good-sized head. Occasionally the nose will be convex. Ears and eyes are attentive. The body is of average length, with muscular hindquarters. The tail is set high. Legs are strong, with clean joints.

The Hackney horse is expected to show a true, four-beat walk. This means that the hind feet extend over the imprints of the forefeet whilst walking. Whilst trotting, the horse has an overstated high knee and hock movement, with good flexion in their joints. The trot should not be rushed. Grace and style is what is required. There is a moment of suspension in the action. Canter is fluid and lilting, whilst the walk is forward-going and elastic.

Pony

The Hackney pony must not exceed 14.2 hands (147cm) but is most often between 12–14 hands (122cm–142.2cm). It is not a miniature version of the Hackney horse, instead showing distinct pony characteristics. It has an alert and intelligent countenance and a muscular, proud physique. It holds its tail high and has a flowing, dynamic, striking movement.

Like the horse, bay is the most usual colour, followed by black. Chestnut is unusual. White markings are common.

The character of the pony is what gets it into the top-tier show rings. They are persistent, brave, enduring and attentive.

Uses

They are driven in harness but can also be shown under saddle or in hand. They are acknowledged as the 'ballerinas of the show ring' with their magnificent high-stepping trot. Other disciplines in which they excel are show-jumping and dressage.

Today

The Rare Breeds Survival Trust categorises the Hackney horse and pony as 'Critical', meaning there are fewer than 300 breeding mares in the UK.

SUFFOLK HORSE

- The breed has the earliest stud book in England, dating from 1877.
- All of these horses are chestnut in colour with no feathering on their legs, making them ideal for working in the heavy, clay, East Anglian soils.
- In 1966, only nine foals were registered with the Suffolk Horse Society.
- 2001 saw the breed regarded as the rarest breed in Britain.

History

The Suffolk horse is also known as the Suffolk Punch or Suffolk Sorrel. It is named after its place of origin: Suffolk in East Anglia, and Punch comes from its heavyweight appearance. The breed is first mentioned in 1586, in William Camden's *Britannia*, where he describes the horse as identical to what we know now, making it the oldest breed of heavy horse existing today. Genetic studies show that the Suffolk Punch is closely related to the Fell and Dale British breeds as well as the European Haflinger.

Agricultural Heritage

The breed was expanded in the sixteenth century, primarily for farm work. They pulled ploughs and took the corn to market, being good tempered and hard workers. Their immense strength, stamina and longevity meant that farmers did not sell them on, so bloodlines were kept pure. There were thousands of them working the land before the First World War. By the time the Second World War occurred, their fate dimmed. Many were slaughtered for meat, and agricultural mechanisation meant steam engines and tractors, well suited to the flat East Anglian countryside, took much of the work away from them.

Crisp's Horse

The breed has the earliest stud book in England, with the Suffolk Horse Society formed in 1877. Crisp's Horse of Ufford (he was unnamed) was foaled in 1768 and many people say that all modern stock descended from him. This is only partially true. The horse belonged to Thomas Crisp who lived near Woodbridge. The stallion was small. He only stood 15.2 hands (157cm) high. What really transpired was a genetic bottleneck in the 1760s, where all other male bloodlines had died out. Further genetic difficulties occured later that century.

Early Influences

In 1784, the average Suffolk Punch was 15 hands (152cm) high. They were strong and compact even then, and were crossed with the Norfolk Trotter and Norfolk Cob, and much later, the Thoroughbred. However, breeding did not change the original character of the Suffolk Punch and it steadfastly remained the same. Its uniform colour is thought to have come from a stallion named Blakes Farmer, foaled in 1760.

Exports

The Punch was exported to Canada in 1865 and to the United States in 1880. The American Suffolk Horse Association produced their first stud book in 1907. The horse was also widely exported to Spain, France, Germany, Austria, Russia, Sweden and areas in Africa, New Zealand, Australia and Argentina to name a few.

Characteristics

The Suffolk Punch now stands about 16.1 to 17.2 hands (165–178cm). They weigh a colossal 900–1,000kg. All of them are chestnut in colour. The word 'chestnut' is used without the middle 't' in this instance. This uniform colour varies from dark liver, dull dark, red and bright chesnut. Any white markings are limited to small parts of the face and lower legs.

The Suffolk Punch has a muscular, curving neck and strong, sloping shoulders with a relatively short back with a powerful, wide croup. It has short, strong legs with no feathering on the fetlocks, making it ideal for working in the East Anglian fields, which are made up of heavy clay soils that could otherwise have clogged up their legs. They are hard workers, maturing early and living long, being inexpensive to keep.

Founding Fathers

The Suffolk Punch was instrumental in the formation of the Jutland breed in Denmark. A Suffolk stallion Oppenheimer LXII, bought into Denmark in the 1860s, was a founding stallion of that breed creating one of its most significant bloodlines. Pakistan imported many Suffolk Punches in the twentieth century creating army horses by mixing them with native horses. The Suffolk has also been important in creating the Vladimir Heavy Draft in the former USSR. Here in Britain, cross-breeding can generate heavy sports horses for hunting or show-jumping.

Critical Status Today

In 1966, there were only nine foals registered with the Suffolk Horse Society, but since then numbers have steadily risen, although the status of the breed remains Critical. By 1998 there were 80 breeding mares in the UK with 40 foals registered. 2001 saw the breed regarded as the rarest breed in Britain. 36 foals were registered in 2007. This number seems to have stabilised as by 2016, there were 30–40 foals registered with a total number of 300 Suffolk Punches in the UK.

ENDANGERED (300 TO 500)

DARTMOOR PONY

- Since the medieval period the ponies have conveyed weighty packs of tin over the moor from the mines.
- Today the pony lives in a semi-feral state on Dartmoor.
- They are known to be kind and steady, making them a perfect child's pony, and are used as a foundation stock for that purpose.

First Tamed 5,500 Years Ago

This native breed has lived on Dartmoor in Devon for centuries. Prehistoric remains have been excavated in chamber tombs of the Vere Gordon Childe's period III–IV in the southern most parts of the UK. They would therefore date to the Neolithic Revolution of 3500BC, when society moved from hunter-gatherer to agriculture. It would have been at this point that the wild ponies were tamed. Further archaeological finds show domestic ponies on the moor from 1500BC. The initial register of ponies on Dartmoor occurs in 1012AD documenting wild animals at Ashburton, as well as memoirs from local manors telling of the branding and ear-marking of these ponies.

Sinclair Photography

Close Neighbours, Distant Genetics

The Exmoor pony does not live far away and is similar in phenotype to the Dartmoor pony. However, they are not deeply affiliated. The Exmoor has an incredibly rare jaw bone which has only otherwise been observed in the prehistoric finds of ponies in Alaska. They have the emergence of a seventh molar, which is not found in any other extant type of horse.

Medieval Tin Mining

Since the medieval period Dartmoor ponies conveyed weighty packs of tin over the moor from the mines. Bloodlines from other breeds have greatly influenced its gene pool, starting with the Shetland, between 1790 and 1840; the idea being the creation of a smaller pit pony. Arab characteristics were received with the stallion Dwarka, foaled in 1922, which was continued by his son, The Leat. Other influences were Welsh pony blood from Dinarth Spark and also Fell pony genetics.

Breed Dynamics over the Centuries

When the mines and quarries fell into disuse, some ponies were kept for farming, but today the pony lives in a semi-feral state on Dartmoor. There were thought to be 25,800 in the 1930s. The Second World War was catastrophic for the breed. The moor itself was utilised for training. The industrialisation of farming further worsened its prospects.

Registration

The initial stud book for the Dartmoor pony was created in 1898 by the Polo Pony Society. The breed society began in 1924, and they established their own stud book. The Second World War saw the registration of only a few ponies, but in the 1950s Dartmoor residents did all they could to inspect and catalogue as many ponies as possible to try and get stud book numbers back up.

The Historic Rights of Dartmoor Commoners

In 1988, the Dartmoor Pony Moorland Scheme was initiated, administered by the Dartmoor Pony Society and the Duchy of Cornwall, in allegiance with Dartmoor National Park. 2004 saw the creation of the Dartmoor Pony Preservation Scheme and the recognition by the RBST of the pony's rare breed standing. All the ponies living on Dartmoor are owned and looked after by Dartmoor residents. Piebald and skewbald ponies living on the moor are not Dartmoor ponies. They are Dartmoor Hill ponies, since the law says that a Dartmoor Commoner may run any pony out on the moor. A Dartmoor Hill pony is grouped as any pony born on the moor. It is illegal to feed a pony on Dartmoor.

Kind and Steady, Ideal for Children

The majority of Dartmoor ponies are from 11.1 to 12.2 hands (114–127cm). According to the breed standard they should not exceed 12.2 hands. Colour ranges from bay to brown, grey, chestnut or roan. There should not be too many white markings. They have small heads with big, gentle eyes and small, pricked up ears. They are of average length with strong, deep girths and muscular hind quarters. They have a full, fluid mane and tail and an effortless, graceful movement. The Dartmoor pony is known to be kind and steady, making it a perfect child's pony, and are used as foundation stock for that purpose. They do have the strength to carry a man and were used in Dartmoor Prison in the beginning of the 1900s for guards accompanying prisoners. Nowadays they can be found in all spheres, including showing, jumping, dressage, driving, hunting and trail riding.

EXMOOR PONY

- They are particularly suited to work that requires stamina and are therefore brilliant at competitive long-distance riding, driving, and excel in agility, winning international titles. They can also be used for dressage and showing, and they love jumping.
- The breed is considered to be Endangered by the RBST meaning the total UK population is less than 500. From this total, there are 300 mares producing 130 foals every year.
- There are 150 mares living 'free' on Exmoor today.

Living Wild on the Moor

The Exmoor pony is one of a number of horse breeds native to Britain. They are traditionally found on Exmoor, an expanse of open moorland in Devon and Somerset in SW England. They are living there wild; finding their own food, nurturing their young and living freely over the moorland. They share a similar conformation to other British mountain and moorland ponies.

For centuries the Exmoor pony lived out in the wild on Exmoor, only being bought in once a year to wean the foals and inspect, brand (with a 4-pointed star), and microchip the newcomers. Enclosure of the moor,

agricultural intensification, the increase in traffic and cross-breeding has led to decreasing numbers in the breed over the last 200 years.

Alaskan Heritage

The remains of two species of horse were found at Pakefield, East Anglia. They are thought to date back to 700,000BC. Fossils, dating from 50,000BC have been unearthed in the Exmoor region. Some claim that the predecessor of all British native ponies travelled from Alaska some 130,000 years ago, spreading throughout the land. During the Ice Age, 9,600 years ago, these pony herds became isolated on mountain and moorland, leading to the different breeds that we enjoy today. However, this theory is uncorroborated by DNA findings although it is notable how close the Exmoor are morphologically to the primitive pony of 60,000 years ago.

Roman Pit Ponies

By 400BC, the ponies were pulling wheeled transport. The Romans mined metals such as tin, iron and copper which were abundant on Exmoor and used the breed as pit ponies. In later centuries, hill farmers would use the ponies for riding whilst tending their flocks, harnessing them for ploughing and harrowing. They would be ridden to feed the farm animals and used for taking the family to market and church.

The Sale of Exmoor Forest and the Creation of the Anchor Herd

It was not until the Doomsday Book in 1086 that we get our first recorded evidence of the ponies on Exmoor. In 1818, the Royal Exmoor Forest was sold by the Crown to John Knight. The departing warden, Sir Thomas Acland, took 30 ponies to privately owned land on Winsford Hill. These were known as the Anchor herd, and some of their descendants can still be found at Winsford Hill. The remaining Exmoor ponies were sold, some going to local breeders where their progeny still live.

Stamina and Endurance in International Fields

Exmoor ponies that are not living semi-feral on the moor are used for a variety of purposes. They are particularly suited to work that requires stamina and are therefore brilliant at competitive long-distance riding and driving, and excel in agility, winning international titles. They can also be used for dressage and showing, and they love jumping. Cross-breeding them with thoroughbreds creates a fantastic hunter. Because they are able to carry a lot of weight for their small size, and they enjoy a long stride, they are also useful for small adults and riders with disabilities.

a Gibson

Conservation Grazing

They have found another niche too in life. That is as a conservation grazer. Their natural hardiness allows the pony to live in a range of habitats, from bogs to high moorland, but they also work well on heathland, chalk grassland and other pasture habitats. They trample the bracken and will eat the tough gorse, purple moor grass, brambles, thistles and soft rushes, leaving space for the more endangered plant species to grow.

Evolutionary Response to a Small Area over a Long Period of Time

The pony is unique in that it has evolved over a long stretch of time, in a small area, answering the challenges of its environment in its development, adapting over the years with characteristics to suit a cold and wet climate. Two features stand out. One is the hooded eye, or extra fleshy eyelid, called 'toad eye' which deflects rainwater away from the face and protects the eyes from extreme weather. The other feature is the 'snow chute', or 'ice tail'; a feature of a group of short, coarse hairs at the dock of the tail, which helps channel rainwater away from the groin and soft under-surface, to the sides of the pony, directing it to a few runoff points at the hind legs. The 'snow chute' is lost every summer to regrow in autumn.

Primitive Colouring

Other features of the pony include pangeré ('mealy') markings around the muzzle, eyes, flanks and under-surface. These are thought to be a primitive characteristic amongst ponies.

The ponies are bay, dun or brown with black points. To enter the breed registry, they are allowed no white markings. Their average height is 11.1–12.3 hands (114–130cm). There is a height limit of 12.2 hands (127cm) for mares, and for stallions and geldings, 12.3 hands (130cm). Some Exmoor ponies, however, reach 13.2 hands (137cm).

Cold Weather Characteristics

The breed is noticeably stocky and powerfully built. They will grow a winter coat, which covers the warm, woolly underfur with long, oily hairs that channel rainwater away from it to various drip off points. The plentiful mane, tail and forelock are also used to channel rain away from the body. Their small, hard feet enable the pony to manage rough terrain. They have a wide girth, so that they can digest large quantities of rough herbage in winter, keeping them warm.

Breeders Unite to form Society

In 1921, the Exmoor Pony Society was established at the Lion Inn in Dulverton. Local breeders and supporters wanted to make sure that the Exmoor pony continued in its pure-bred form amidst various dangers. Ponies were inspected for several years by expert breeders and a stud book was launched in 1963.

Children's Story

The ponies enjoyed a wave of publicity in the 1930s due to the publication of the children's book, *Moorland Mousie*, which tells the story of an Exmoor pony.

Genetic Diversity threatened by Small Number of Ponies

The breed is considered to be Endangered by the Rare Breeds Survival Trust, meaning that the total UK population is fewer than 500. In 2010, there were thought to be 800 Exmoor ponies across the globe. From this total, there are 300 mares producing 130 foals every year. There are 150 mares living 'free' on Exmoor today. However, due to the lack of existing bloodlines, there are concerns regarding genetic diversity.

Vulnerable (500 to 900)

Clydesdale Horse

- Exports were huge, with 20,183 horses recorded as going abroad between 1884 and 1945. They were especially popular in Australia and were credited as being the 'horses that built Australia'.
- The breed became famous when the US lifted its prohibition laws in 1933 and Clydesdale horses were employed to dispatch the initial keg of beer from the brewery in St Louis.
- A single Clydesdale can pull in the region of 1,800kg, nearly two tonnes.
- They are now well known for their role as drum horses in the Household Cavalry.

Recorded from 1826

The Clydesdale horse originated in Clydesdale, a county of Scotland, now known as Lanarkshire, home to the River Clyde. Two men, John Paterson of Lochlyloch and the 6th Duke of Hamilton, imported some Flemish stallions and bred them with the native draught mares. Shire horse blood was later used to increase the height of the animals and give them their characteristic feathering in their legs. The first recorded use of the term 'Clydesdale' was in 1826 at an exhibition in Glasgow. By 1830, with written records from 1837, stallions were hired throughout Scotland and northern England if they won a prize at agricultural improvement shows. The winning stallion would be taken throughout the region, mating with the mares. This system amalgamated the Scottish draught horse with the Clydesdale by 1840. 1877 saw the formation of the Clydesdale Horse Society of Scotland, with the American Clydesdale Association, (representing both the US and Canada), following in 1879. At the peak, there were 140,000 working farm horses of Clydesdale origin with an unidentified number in urban environments.

The 'Horses that Built Australia'

Exports were huge. 1,617 stallions left the UK in 1911, with 20,183 horses recorded as going abroad between 1884 and 1945. These stallions, mares and fillies were sent to North and South America, Russia, Italy, Austria, Australia and New Zealand. They were especially popular in Australia, becoming the

dominant draught breed, and were credited with being the 'horses that built Australia'. The Commonwealth Clydesdale Horse Society was formed in 1918 to celebrate that achievement. However, fortunes were to waver. The First World War saw a lot of the horses and their owners go off to war, and the increased need for food production saw the mechanisation of farming. The horses were not required anymore. In 1949, the number of stallions had dropped to 80, compared to 200 in 1946 – only three years earlier.

Prohibition and the Household Cavalry

However, the breed had become famous in 1933 as the US lifted its prohibition laws and Clydesdale horses were employed to dispatch the initial kegs of beer from the brewery at St Louis. A single Clydesdale can pull in the region of 1,800kg, nearly two tonnes. They have immense strength and stamina with high-stepping, showy paces and are still used in agriculture and logging as well as for driving, riding and showing. They are now well known as drum horses for the Household Cavalry, performing on ceremonial and state events, carrying the Musical Ride Officer and two drums, each weighing 56kg. Their calm nature, and their ability to learn quickly, makes them exceptionally qualified for this role. This ritual has been copied throughout the world.

One Tonne Horses

The Clydesdale stands in the region of 16 to 18 hands (163–183cm). They weigh 820 to 910kg, although some large males can be up to 1,000kg and stand over 18 hands. They have a straight, occasionally protuberant nose, with large ears and an arching, lengthy neck with a broad muzzle. Defined withers lead onto a short back, with sloping shoulders and a muscular, strong body. There is prolific feathering on their lower legs, and they have an energetic gait, cleanly lifting their hooves giving the appearance of power and class. The Clydesdale comes in a range of colours – black, grey, a roan pattern, and occasionally chestnut, although bay is the most common. Colouring is often a more desirable characteristic than other physical traits and it is thought that sabino genetics cause the roan body colourings and excessive white markings. As a result, Clydesdales are selectively bred to create the desired colour.

FELL PONY

- The Fell pony is thought to have derived from the now extinct Galloway pony of Scotland, which was used in the Border raids of England.
- The Fell pony had its work cut out for it in the eleventh and twelfth centuries as it had varied uses, such as long journeys carrying fleeces, woollen items, cheese, meat and other foods, and as well as regional metal ores.
- The thirteenth century saw an increased systematic wool traffic to Belgium, which suited the Fell pony as it could cope with large loads over long periods of time: up to 240 miles (390km) per week.
- In the north-east the ponies were used in the big collieries right into the twentieth century.

Ancestral Border Raids

The Fell pony originated in the north of England, probably before the Romans arrived, in what was Cumberland and Westmorland (now Cumbria) and Northumberland. They are thought to have derived from the now extinct Galloway pony of Scotland, which was used in the Border raids of England. The Fell pony is closely comparable to the Dales pony which also originates from the Pennines.

Roman Stallions

In terms of equine history, ponies ranged the UK from pre-historic times. By the Iron Age, ponies of around 12.1 hands were regularly used throughout the country. It was not until the Romans arrived and developed British breeds that ponies of 13 hands were more common. It is not known whether Roman stallions were used to improve the Fell pony but it cannot be ruled out.

Guarding Against Wolves in the Twelfth Century

Later on, the Vikings utilised the Fell pony agriculturally, for ploughing and pack work as well as for drawing sledges and for riding. The Fell pony had its work cut out in the eleventh and twelfth centuries as it had varied uses, such as long journeys carrying fleeces, woollen items, cheese, meat and other food, and regional metal ores. Other uses included looking after the sheep and guarding against wolves.

Pit Ponies in the Industrial Revolution

The thirteenth century saw an increased systematic wool traffic to Belgium, which suited the Fell pony as it was a strong and steady mover, with a calm nature and could cope with large loads over long periods of time: up to 390km per week. The Fell pony carried on as a pack horse throughout the Middle Ages up until the eighteenth century. The Industrial Revolution saw the production of iron, copper and lead in north-west of England. In the north-east the ponies were used in the big collieries right into the twentieth century, working underground if there was enough room, and overground transporting machinery and bringing food from the towns to the pits. Canals and railways soon became the predominant methods of moving goods, but the Fell ponies continued in their pack work and became part of the postal service, able to reach even isolated neighbourhoods.

Retaining Characteristics rather than Improving

The first registrations of the Fell pony were in the Polo and Riding Pony stud book in 1898. The Fell Pony Committee became a Society in 1916, retaining

the old characteristics of the pony rather than improving it. Numbers of the Fell pony were falling by 1945 when a breeding programme and grading up system were introduced. This continued until 1970, but it was the prosperous 1950s that saw the increase in riding for pleasure that really helped Fell pony and other native breed numbers.

Carrying the Queen's Favour

Nowadays, the Fell pony is used for riding and driving. Some compete in endurance riding and the Cumbrian trotting races. Others perform shepherding and pony treks, carrying equipment to mend hiking paths that would be hard for tractors to reach. In Scotland these ponies carry the stags and grouse panniers from the hills. The Queen has a few ponies for this use and has other Fell ponies for riding and driving. The Fell pony is extremely popular for its reliable nature and practical build. The charity, Riding for the Disabled, have quite a few. The Fell Pony Society have a yearly endurance competition where ponies have to work over rough and boggy ground, with various hazards placed in their path. Fell ponies are best seen in working hunter classes. They are ideal for Pony Club and are an all-round, multifaceted family pony.

Cistercian Monks Introducing the Grey Pony to Show Monastic Ownership

The pony stands 13.2 hands (137cm) on average, although it does reach 14 hands (142cm). Early stud books show the most predominant colour to be brown, although black has superseded that in the last few decades. Bay and grey are also acceptable colours. It is thought that the Cistercian monks created the grey colouration as 'white' ponies showed that they belonged to the monastery. Chestnuts, piebalds, and skewbalds are not acceptable and only a white star on the head, and a little white on or below the hind fetlock is allowed. Today, there are herds of Fell ponies on the Cumbrian hills, keeping the breed's characteristics of stamina, sure-footedness and resourcefulness alive.

HIGHLAND PONY

- The Highland pony is one of three native equine breeds of Scotland's Highlands and Islands.
- The Highland is one of the biggest mountain and moorland pony varieties in the UK.
- The Highland pony is incredibly hardy and able to cope with the strong and often severe weather conditions in the Scottish Highlands.
- Frequently, primitive markings such as a dorsal stripe and zebra markings on the legs and shoulder are seen.
- A small white star is allowed by the breed standard, but absolutely no other white markings. Stallions showing white markings, other than the star, are not suitable for licensing.

One of the Biggest Mountain and Moorland Ponies

The Highland pony is one of three native equine breeds of Scotland's Highlands and Islands. The other two are the Eriskay pony and the Shetland pony. The Highland is one of the biggest mountain and moorland pony varieties in the UK. There were originally two types – the smaller ponies found on the Western Islands and the larger ponies of the mainland. Over time, both combined, and there is very little variation nowadays. However, the characteristics of the smaller pony can still be found in the Eriskay pony.

The Highland Pony Society

Introduction of Other Breeds in the sixteenth and nineteenth century

The sixteenth century saw Spanish and French breeds, such as the Percheron,

mixing with the Highland pony. It is also thought that breeds such as the Norfolk Roadster and the Arab may have had some input. Later, in the nineteenth century, Hackney, Fell and Dales ponies were also run with the Highland. Breeding records have been kept since the 1880s.

Croft Work

The Highland pony has evolved to be incredibly hardy and able to cope with the strong and often severe weather conditions in the Scottish Highlands. The ponies very rarely need rugs, even today. In the past, their work consisted of lugging timber and game, and also ploughing on the small farms where they lived. They are still used to take deer carcasses down from the hills, with specially created saddles.

Good All-Rounders

Other uses today include pony trekking, which is said to have been established by Ewan Ormiston at Badenoch near Newtonmore in 1952, using Highland ponies and whose descendants make up the existing herd there today. Ponies being utilised in croft work are rare nowadays, although that was their traditional use. They are much more likely to be found riding and jumping, and are good all-round ponies. They are also used for logging in areas where machines cannot reach as their pony hooves do comparatively little damage.

They have furthermore found work in conservation grazing, especially in regions of extreme weather. They seldom need shoeing and are incredibly inexpensive to maintain. They have an innate hardiness coupled with a very kind temperament.

Flowing Tails and Silky Feathering

The Highland pony stands between 13 to 14.2 hands (132–147cm). They have a well carried head, with a large jowl and neat ears. They should have an alert expression with a gentle eye. They are well balanced and compact, with a great deal of power in their hindquarters and a good-sized chest, allowing for a strong heart and lungs. They have some silky feathering behind the fetlocks. In showing ponies, the mane and tail must be flowing and untrimmed. In the past, when the ponies lived out on the hills, their tails would be kept in shape naturally by brushing against vegetation, but today, trimming some hair from the bottom of the tail is allowed in the interests of safety.

Colour Changes

The Highland pony comes in a variety of colours, including a range of duns: mouse, yellow, grey and cream. It is also found in grey, black, bay and rarely liver chestnut with a silver mane and tail. Frequently, primitive markings such as a dorsal stripe and zebra markings on the legs and shoulder are seen. Foals commonly change colour, as do ponies as they mature, particularly if their originally colour is mixed with grey hairs. There can be a colour change between seasons as the coarse winter coat is shed in spring for a lighter summer coat underneath. However, broken colours are not allowed by the breed standard, including piebald and skewbald. A small white star is allowed, but absolutely no other white markings and the hooves are required to be black. Stallions showing white markings, other than the star, are not suitable for licensing.

AT RISK (900 TO 1500)

NEW FOREST PONY

- Ponies have been found in the New Forest since the end of the last Ice Age. Fossil evidence found locally, showing a spear wound on a pony's shoulder, has been dated to 500,000BC.
- William the Conqueror, when he seized the Crown of England in 1066, instigated the New Forest for use as a royal hunting ground.
- Some local people, known as the 'Commoners', have common grazing rights to the Forest.
- The 1850s and 60s saw the use of Arab blood to improve the New Forest pony, but this did not have the desired effect.
- New Forest ponies were utilised during the Boer War in South Africa.

500,000BC Spear Wound

Ponies have been found in the New Forest since the end of the last Ice Age. Fossil evidence, showing a spear wound on a pony's shoulder, has been found at Eartham Pit in Boxgrove, only 50 miles from the Forest. This pony was alive in 500,000BC. Ringwood, on the west of the Forest, was home to a sizable Ice Age hunting camp. Iron Age excavations near Danebury, 25 miles from the Forest, show the horses were about 12 hands high (122cm), akin to today. DNA studies show a common ancestry with the endangered Celtic-type pony breeds, the Asturcón, and the Pottock, from Spain.

William the Conqueror seized the Crown, and instigated the New Forest as a Royal Hunting Ground

It was William the Conqueror who brought with him at least 2,000 horses from France when he seized the Crown of England in 1066, and instigated the New Forest for use as a royal hunting ground. It was then that the system of rights of common pasture were afforded to the local people. There is a popular myth that Spanish stallions swam ashore during the Spanish Armada and set about breeding with the native ponies, but the Spanish blood is said to have come from a Royal Stud set up in Lyndhurst in 1507, where offspring were sent off to the Renaissance wars.

Stock

Thoroughbred Roots

One early stallion, Marske, that had great influence on the New Forest breed was owned by Prince William, Duke of Cumberland. When the Duke died in October 1765, a Ringwood farmer purchased the horse for 20 guineas. Marske was a thoroughbred, great-grandson of the famous Darley Anderson and father of Eclipse – another notable horse. Marske was run with the mares in the forest during the 1760s.

Arab Blood creates Prize-Winning Races

The 1850s and 60s saw the use of Arab blood to improve the New Forest pony, but this did not have the desired effect. The ponies became unsuitable as pit ponies and their reduced hardiness meant that they were finding the winters in the Forest difficult. However, as a consequence of the Arab blood, during the nineteenth century there was money to be made! Races were regularly held and prize money was £5 to £10, at a time when a man might earn £1 a week. The winning ponies were usually gelded, so that they could carry on racing. As a result, the quality of stock decreased over time. These ponies were also highly valued as harness ponies, being outstanding trotters.

Boer War ponies

New Forest ponies were utilised during the Boer War in South Africa, surpassing the standard ponies by carrying 180 pounds or 13 stone continually through the day in severe heat. On their return, they shone again, with a New Forest Pony winning the Army Jumping Prize in Aldershot. By the Second World War, many of these ponies were being slaughtered for horse meat.

From 1930, No More Improving, Only Preserving

Two separate societies promoting the improvement of the New Forest pony merged in 1937 to create the New Forest Pony Breeding and Cattle Society. They prevented the inclusion of other native breeds, such as the Fell, Dartmoor, Exmoor, Dales and Highland, which had been used to increase hardiness and other indigenous traits. From 1930 onwards, only purebred New Forest stallions were allowed to run with the mares. A purebred horse being one that has both parents registered as purebred in the studbook. The stud book has been published since 1960, and New Forest ponies exported to North America, Europe and Australia also possess their own breed associations and stud registers.

'Architects of the Forest'

Some local people, known as the Commoners, have common grazing rights to the Forest, allowing cattle, donkeys, pigs and sheep, as well as the ponies, to graze the 37,550 hectares of open Forest. These animals have created the eco-system of the Forest as we know it, with more than a thousand years of grazing, clearing away undergrowth and allowing room for flowers, birds and other flora and fauna. They are known as 'the Architects of the Forest'. The Commoners will pay an annual amount per animal that is living semi-feral. The animals are watched over by five Agisters: one in each region of the Forest and one overall Agister, who will then report to the Verderers of the New Forest. This is an ancient role going back to the thirteenth century when it is thought the Verderers held court in the New Forest, licensed by the Crown. Now their role is shared with the Forestry Commission and National park authority.

Limiting the Breeding

At this time, most ponies turned out on the Forest are mares, and live in small groups, with a leading mare, her daughters and their foals. Stallions are allowed to run with them, but to a timetable, to ensure that foals are born after the spring grass has emerged and before it gets too cold. This usually means they are out from May to August, and their numbers are limited to around 50; less during periods of financial hardship. Colts are judged when they are two years old for their suitability to be used as stallions.

Drifts and Agisters

Drifts take place throughout the autumn, with a quality check on the animals in each Agister's care. Some owners decide to keep their ponies in over the winter. The majority of the colts and a few of the fillies are withdrawn. Excess animals are sold at the Beaulieu Road Pony Sales, administered by the New Forest Livestock Society. Each Agister marks the ponys' tails in a slightly different way to indicate depasturing fees have been settled, whilst ear tags are used for cattle. Foals are branded and ponies are wormed. The Agister will keep an eye on the ponies for the rest of the year, but apart from troublesome animals, which will need to be removed, the ponies are left to their own devices unless they need a vet or supplementary food, in which case they will probably be withdrawn from the Forest. Ponies wander freely along the roads, and although they have the right of way over cars, there are several accidents each year.

Sure-Footed and Quick to Learn

There is no minimum standard height for the New Forest pony, although they are usually at least 12 hands high (122cm). The maximum height allowed is 14.2 hands (148cm). They are described as a solid working type, being quick to learn, with an even, sure-footed, active gait showing no exaggeration. They have a solid confirmation with sloping shoulders and robust hindquarters. Larger ponies, whilst able to carry adults, are narrow enough to support a child. Colours are mostly bay, chestnut or grey. Piebald and skewbald are disallowed, as well as the blue-eyed cream type. Very light chestnut and palomino ponies are only permitted on the stud book as mares and geldings. The only white markings allowed are those on the head and lower leg.

Boxing Day Race

There is a race in the New Forest every year on Boxing Day, where the meeting place is only disclosed to riders on the evening before. The start point is published when riders arrive. The point to point terminates at a different place each year, and there is no set route, so those riders who know the Forest best have the edge. New Forest ponies are used today in eventing, driving, gymkhanas, cross-country, show jumping and dressage.

SHIRE HORSE

- The Shire was originally used as a war horse in medieval times.
- Coach springs were on the market in 1690, and a large muscular horse was needed to pull coaches over the appalling roads of the time.
- The late eighteenth century saw improvements in the canals, allowing the movement of large loads across the country. The Shire horse fitted this role perfectly.
- During the Second World War there were tight regulations on the use of animal feed, leading to thousands of Shires being butchered.

The Original War Horse

The largest horse ever registered was a Shire called Mammoth who was born in 1848. He was 21.25 hands high (219cm) and weighed 1,524kg. The history of the horse goes back thousands of years, with the first evidence of their close relationship with humans shown by late Bronze Age graves containing remnants of bridles. The Shire was originally used as a war horse in medieval times, and was known as the Great Horse, as it carried heavily armoured knights into battle. During the reign of King Henry VIII, from 1509–1547, no stallion under 15 hands was allowed. The development of gunpowder saw the decline of the Shire in the battlefield. As armour became less heavy, Oliver Cromwell's horsemen, during his rule from 1653-1658, preferred a smaller, swifter horse.

Big Horse for Bad Roads

The Shire horses were redundant, but found a use in draught work, ousting what was the oxen's original job. Shire horses had been sold at Smithfield Market in London from 1145 as 'fit for the dray, the plough, or the chariot'. The Shire's gentle nature and enormous strength meant that they were able to pull carts and move goods. They were smaller than the Shires of today, and it was during the sixteenth century that Dutch engineers, employed to drain the English fens, brought Friesian horses that significantly improved the breed. Coach springs were on the market in 1690, and a large, muscular horse, with great big hooves, was needed to pull coaches over the appalling roads of the time. Again, technology caught up with the Shire, and developments in coach construction and advances in road design meant that lighter, faster horses could be utilised.

Carol Stevens

Flanders Improvement

Also in the seventeenth century, Robert Bakewell was designing some horses using six Dutch and Flanders mares. He was improving the Old English Black Horse with its direct links to the Medieval battle horses. He came up with two lines, the Fen or Lincolnshire, and the Leicester or Midlands variety. They were both black. It was not until the mid-seventeenth century that the term 'Shire horse' was instigated, with records being produced by the late eighteenth century. Many consider the 'Packington Blind Horse' from Leicestershire to be the foundation sire of the Shire breed. He was available for stud from 1755 to 1770.

Transportation Giants

The late eighteenth century saw improvements in the canals, allowing the movement of large loads across the country. The Shire horse again fitted this role perfectly. The development of the railway system could have meant a decline in the Shire population, but they were utilised to transport goods to and from the yards, and indeed, in 1893 there were 6,000 registered heavy horses being used for this purpose. It is estimated that, at this time, there were 19,000 heavy horses in London hauling goods, whilst a further 1,500 would have been used to clear up London's rubbish. In this same year, 1893, 3,000 heavy horses were used by London breweries for deliveries. A great many of these horses would have been Shires.

First Stud Book in 1878 with Records Going Back to 1770

The English Cart Horse Society was formed in 1878, becoming the Shire Horse Society in 1884. The first stud book was published in its inaugural year of 1878, with known lineages going back to 1770. Shires were exported to the US in 1853, with the American Shire Horse Association created in 1885.

Second World War Regulations lead to Shires being Butchered

The twentieth century was not so kind. The Second World War saw tight regulations on the use of livestock feed, leading to thousands of Shires being butchered and leading studs shut down. Increased mechanisation in cars and tractors took away work from the Shire. Numbers fell from over a million horses in their heyday to only a few thousand by 1960.

Two Shires Pull 45 Tonnes

According to the Shire Horse Society in the UK, stallions must be 17 hands (178cm) or over. Geldings can be smaller, from 16.2 hands (168cm) and mares must be at least 16 hands (163cm). Weight ranges for the males are from 850–1,100kg: that's a one tonne horse. Two Shires, in 1924, managed to pull between them a load of 45 tonnes. Shires can be black, bay, grey or roan, except the stallion, who cannot be roan or have excessive white markings. Introduction of Clydesdale blood in the 1950s and 60s, changed the leg feathering from coarse to silky. Shires have a long neck and face, with large eyes. They have deep, broad shoulders and chest. Their back is short with long, powerful hindquarters.

An Environmental Option for Forestry

Nowadays, Shires are kept for forestry – their large feet are less ruinous to the environment than a tractor. This can also be useful for harrowing sports fields and river beds. Ploughing matches are held around the country and are an enjoyable day out. Heavy Horse Centres and working farms show the Shire off in its natural environment, and a Shire can be hired for weddings and carnivals. Breweries, such as the Hook Norton Brewery in Oxfordshire, and the Samuel Smith Brewery in Tadcaster, still use the Shire to deliver their beer. The revival of the Shire means we are also not losing traditional skills, such as harness manufacture, heavy horse farriery and other techniques.

PIGS

ENDANGERED
(100 TO 200 BREEDING FEMALES)

British Landrace
British Lop
Large Black
Middle White

VULNERABLE
(200 TO 300)

Berkshire
Large White
Tamworth

AT RISK
(300 TO 500)

British Saddleback
Gloucester Old Spots
Oxford Sandy and Black
Welsh

ENDANGERED
(100 TO 200 BREEDING FEMALES)

BRITISH LANDRACE

- Pigs give off a pheromone in their saliva. This is to signal that they want to mate. The male will release this steroid, which sends the female pigs wild!
- Over 90 per cent of all hybrid gilts in Western Europe and North America come from the Landrace.
- As a result, the British Landrace is known as the 'Universal Breed'.
- Despite the popularity of the British Landrace, its use in hybridisation has created a shortfall, and purebred British Landrace pigs are very difficult to find today.
- The RBST lists them as 'Endangered', meaning that there are only 100–200 breeding sows registered in the UK today.

Initial Imports

The Landrace pig was first imported into the UK in 1949, with four boars (uncastrated males) and eight gilts (female pig that has not yet had piglets) arriving in Northern Ireland, the Isle of Man and the Channel Islands, from Sweden. Further imports followed in 1953. Denmark faced export restrictions on their Landrace pigs until 1950, as they were attempting to protect their export market in bacon.

1955 Hewitt Report

The British Landrace was amongst the Welsh pig and Large White pig in being selected by the government to focus efforts on food production after the Second World War. The 1955 Howitt report, which recommended the emphasis on these three breeds, inadvertently created a downfall in the population of many other British breeds. Indeed, it is reported that seven pig breeds were lost in the UK during the twentieth century.

Pig Testing Scheme

The British Landrace Pig Society was created in 1950, and a herd book was started. Pigs were assessed under the initiatory Pig Testing Scheme which

measured daily gain and fat depths at an assessment centre, purpose built at Stockton-on-Forest, near York. This station led the way in commercial and pedigree pig farming. 1950 also saw the creation of the American Landrace Association.

Herd Book

With the need to join forces with other pig breeds and the creation of a national herd book, in 1978 the British Landrace Pig Society connected with the National Pig Breeders' Association (NPBA), which later became the British Pig Association.

New Bloodlines and the Creation of a Breed

Encouraged by their success, the 1980s saw further imports, with different bloodlines coming into England, Scotland and Northern Ireland from Norway. Northern Ireland also imported from Finland and carried on importing from Norway. These new bloodlines were very important. After examination, they were bred with existing swine to create a wider genetic foundation. This expansion of genetics created the new breed of British Landrace which stood out from other Landrace pigs found around the globe.

Global Hybridisation

The British Landrace has found immense popularity amongst farmers. Testing still continues, with improvements being made, to keep up the ever-increasing standards of modern commercial and pedigree farming. The Landrace is renowned for improving other pig breeds. Ninety per cent of hybrid gilt production in the West of Europe and North America use Landrace pigs to produce the quality of meat that we enjoy today. Not to mention the increased profits this brings to the farmers.

Characteristics

The British Landrace is a medium to large, white pig with occasional (undesired) black spots. It has heavy drooping ears that hide the majority of its face, hence being defined as lop-eared. It is an adaptable breed, working well both indoors and outdoors. Sows are good mothers, with large litters, ranging from 6–10 piglets, with 2–3 litters per annum.

Teeth and Gut

Piglets are born with 28 teeth which they lose at 12 months. They are replaced by the adult set of 44 teeth, which will be covered with enamel, like humans, which helps to protect the mouth from disease. The pigs chew their food, again, like humans, as they share a similar digestive system. Their lungs are comparatively small compared to their body size.

Sexual Saliva

Pigs give off a pheromone in their saliva. This is to signal that they want to mate. The male will release this steroid, which sends the female pigs wild! A British Landrace is known to drink 14 gallons of water per day. They have a superb sense of smell and their snout is vital in foraging for food. They are remarkably clean and even piglets will find a toilet area, well away from their bedding.

The breed can be seen apart from the Large White as the latter has erect ears, a concave face and deeper sides. Large Whites, as their name suggests, are bigger than the British Landrace. Pigs are omnivores, in that they eat both meat and plants.

Uses

British Landrace piglets are known to have a good daily gain, with quick early growth, and high lean meat content, in a brilliantly fleshed carcass. The British Landrace carries more fat than the Large White, so is used predominantly for bacon. They do not produce so many piglets as the Large White, but they have the biggest piglets once they have finished weaning.

The British Landrace has the third fastest rate of growth. Their carcasses are noted to be long. The average weight of a fully grown sow is 204–272kg. A mature boar will weigh 226–318kg.

Today

As mentioned before, over 90 per cent of all hybrid gilts in Western Europe and North America come from British Landrace bloodlines. As a result, the pig is known as the 'Universal Breed'. The British Landrace is still crossed with Scandinavian breeds to improve its characteristics.

Despite the popularity of the British Landrace, its use in hybridisation has created a shortfall, and purebred British Landrace pigs are very difficult to find today. The Rare Breeds Survival Trust lists them as Endangered, meaning that there are only 100–200 breeding sows registered in the UK today.

BRITISH LOP EARED PIG

- Unlike many breeds, the British Lop was not bred with Asian pigs, which aimed at improving the quality of meat.
- It is listed by the RBST as Rare. Although this listing generally encourages more people to own a British Lop, the breed has suffered for not looking particularly beautiful.
- The British Lop is very docile and easy to manage in spite of its size. It is an excellent mother and prolific breeder. Litters of 12–14 piglets are normal.
- Without the commitment of a handful of breeders, this pig would be extinct.
- The late celebrity chef, Clarissa Dickson Wright, a great fan of the breed, was right in saying that 'the British Lop is rarer than the Giant Panda'.

No Asian Influence

The British Lop Eared pig is a West Country breed, first recognised in Tavistock and is sometimes called the Devon Lop or Cornish White pig. It is probably linked to comparable breeds living in north-west Europe, particularly the Welsh Pig and the Landrace pigs found in Scandinavia. The Normande pigs of France also share certain similarities. It lived in the south-west of England until the twentieth century, rarely being found past Somerset or Devon. Unlike many breeds, it was not bred with Asian pigs, which aimed at improving the quality of meat. Instead it carried on, eating sparsely from otherwise unproductive land.

Recognition at Last!

The first herd book for the species was published in 1921, after successful classes at the Devon Country Show. Its popularity continued into the late 1930s where a large number of British Lop Eared pigs were registered, mainly in the SW. However, numbers fell in the 1960s and '70s with only 11 breeders recognised in the country. The 1960s saw a name change from the National Long White Lop Eared pig to the British Lop Eared pig we know today.

Political Downfall

At the end of the Second World War in 1945, rationing meant that food production in the UK needed to be increased. The 1947 Agricultural Act stated that 'The twin pillars upon which the Government's agricultural policy rests are stability and efficiency'. The highly influential Howitt report of October 1955 led to the consequential decision to focus pig production on only three,

Bob Berry

more commercially feasible, breeds of pig. The three breeds that were chosen to concentrate on were the Large White, the Landrace and the Welsh pig. This was a catastrophe for the British Lop. Now deemed insignificant, breeding was continued by only very few farmers in the south-west. Numbers fell and the breed became very rare.

Not Good Looking enough to be Noticed

Today, the British Lop is still very scarce, although herds have spread from the SW to the rest of the country. The RBST, when it was founded in 1973, listed the British Lop as one of six pig breeds that it listed as Rare. Although this listing generally encourages more people to own a British Lop, the breed has suffered for not looking particularly beautiful; not having a short snout, ginger or spotted markings that other pig breeds do. To the amateur eye, it could easily be mistaken for a Welsh or Landrace pig, although the British Lop is much deeper in the body.

Easy Breeding

The British Lop is very docile and easy to manage in spite of their size. It is an excellent mother and prolific breeder. Litters of 12–14 piglets are normal. It has a pure white skin, with long, white hair and no grey markings or wrinkles. The pig has a large frame, with a straight, level back and deep body. Its tail is set high up and it has long, thin ears that fall forward over the face, reaching over to the end of the nose.

Commitment and Contempt

There are only eight genetic lines left, with less than 360 breeding sows and fewer than 100 boars. The pig was highly favoured by Queen Victoria and was once known as the 'Royal Pig', but it is not popular with commercial farmers. Without the commitment of a handful of breeders, this pig would be extinct.

Worrying Statistics

The breed society was formed in 1918, keeping an independent herd book. The RBST still have this animal listed as Endangered. The late Clarissa Dickson Wright, a great fan of the breed, said that 'the British Lop is rarer than the Giant Panda'. She was right; there are approximately 1,140 Giant Pandas left in the world from January 2019, compared to 321 registered British Lop Eared pigs. (This figure comprises 54 bulls and 267 sows).

LARGE BLACK

- In 1919, a Large Black Sow won Supreme Champion at Smithfield and was thereupon sold for 700 guineas.
- The Large Black was a very popular export pig. They were selected instead of Berkshire pigs. Black skin helps a pig cope with sunburn. Additionally, they had excellent scavenging capacities and superior reproductive rates.
- Between 1940 and 1952, one Large Black sow produced 26 litters, and entered the Guinness Book of Records for the highest number of litters ever recorded for a pig.
- They are good when killed at a lower weight, as pork, but are best when killed at a higher weight, and traditionally cured as bacon.
- There is a growing demand for meat from traditional breeds raised on an extensive farming system.

Old English Hog

The Large Black is uniquely the only completely black breed of pig in the UK. It developed from the Old English Hog found in the sixteenth and seventeenth centuries. The English agriculturist, Richard Parkinson, notably said in 1810: 'They are distinguished by their gigantic size, they are the largest of the kind I have ever seen, and as perfect a make as possible in pigs; their heads are large, with very long ears hanging down on each side of the face, so they can scarcely see their way'.

Two Strains

The Large Black is also known as the Devon, Cornwall Black, or Boggu. In the late 1880s there were two defined strains of Large Black, one found in Devon and Cornwall, and the other in East Anglia. The West Country variety were very similar to pigs found in Europe but most especially France. The East Anglian variety were thought to be modified by Chinese imports in the late eighteenth century.

Black Essex, Black Suffolk and Small Black

The popularity of the breed grew throughout the late nineteenth century and in 1898–9 the Large Black Pig Society was formed in Ipswich in Suffolk, with a herd book coming out in 1899. East Anglian breeds, such as the Black Essex, Black Suffolk, Small Black and others, were widely crossed with the Devon and Cornwall strains so that by 1913 'general uniformity' was the norm.

T

Supreme Champion sells for 700 guineas

Into the twentieth century, the breed found popularity across the country. It was widely crossed with Large Whites and Middle Whites to instigate good bacon and pork pigs. In 1919, a Large Black sow won Supreme Champion at Smithfield and was thereupon sold for 700 guineas. That same year, 121 Large Blacks were entered at the Royal Show – more than any other breed.

Sunburn Survival Skills

The Large Black was a very popular export pig. They were selected instead of Berkshire pigs. Both have black skin which helps a pig cope with sunburn. Additionally, the Large Black had excellent scavenging capacities and superior reproductive rates. Australia saw their first arrivals in 1902 or 1903 and by 1935 this breed had been exported to more than 35 countries.

Effect of the Second World War

Such popularity was short lived and after the Second World War, farmers began to turn to pigs that would do well in an intensive system. The Large Black Pig Society was amalgamated with the National Pig Breeders' Association (now the British Pig Association) in 1949.

The 1955 Howitt report was catastrophic for the Large Black. Pig farming in the UK was not as productive as in Europe. It was felt that the diversity of local breeds did not help. so decided to concentrate on just three breeds – the British Landrace, the Welsh and the Large White. It pushed traditional breeds to the margins, and many died out. The Rare Breeds Survival Trust, which was formed in 1973, categorised the Large Black as Endangered. The American Livestock Breeds Conservancy, the Rare Breeds Trust of Australia and Rare Breeds Canada also have the Large Black on their critical list.

Characteristics

The Large Black pig has very long ears, which hang over its face, often impairing its ability to see. It is a deep bodied, hardy pig suitable for extensive farming. Due to their advanced rootling about and browsing they thrive on pastures where they convert low grade feed into meat. This characteristic makes them unsuitable for intensive farming. They are the only fully black pig in the UK. They are a submissive breed of pig and are quite easily contained by two strands of electric fencing.

Fertility

The Large Black sow is fertile with strong maternal instincts. The average number of piglets in a litter is 8.56, but the range is usually from 8–10. Thirteen piglets in a litter have been known. Between 1940 and 1952, one Large Black sow produced 26 litters, and entered the Guinness Book of Records for the highest number of litters ever recorded for a pig.

Weight

The weight of a boar is around 320–360kg and a sow, 270–320kg. An overweight sow can sometimes have cystic ovaries, which stops her breeding. In the 1900s the average weight for sows was 230kg, and more for a boar – showing that the breed has increased in weight over the years.

Uses

The Large Black has delicious meat. It is good when killed at a lower weight, as pork, but is at its best when killed at a higher weight, then traditionally cured as bacon. The meat has a lean quality and good flavour lacking surplus fat. In the past it was bred with the Yorkshire and Middle White to give rise to a powerful hybrid. Today, its fortunes are not so good, as commercial producers do not like the black skin of the purebred pig. However, its use in producing Parma Ham is beginning to make the pig more popular again, and there is a growing demand for meat from traditional breeds raised on an extensive farming system.

Conservation Status

In 1954 the UK pig population stood at approximately 65,000, with 3.4 per cent of this Large Black pigs. There were 2,195 in total, consisting of 269 licensed boars and 1926 registered sows. 2011 figures report 421 Large Blacks in total, with 86 boars and 335 sows, making it one of the rarest historic pig breed in the UK. The British Pig Association inform us that there are six recognised boar lines and 24 sow lines on record in the UK. Figures for the rest of the world are not so promising either. In the US they report 300 breeding sows and a worldwide total of 2,000 Large Blacks.

In 2019, the Rare Breeds Survival Trust recognises the Large Black pig as Endangered, with between 100 and 200 breeding sows registered in the UK.

MIDDLE WHITE

- The Middle White developed from crossing the Large White with the Small White.
- The dished face of the Middle White, along with the characteristic pricked ears and short snout all originate from Chinese and Siamese pigs which were bred with the Small White.
- The breed was extremely popular in London as was fondly known as 'the London Porker'.
- The Second World War bought a reversal of fortunes, as rationing led to a decline in 'pork' breeds, favouring 'bacon' breeds.
- The pig is hardy but requires refuge in acute temperatures.
- According to 2009 research, litters average at 8.99 piglets.

Creation of a New Breed

The Middle White came into existence as a breed purely by chance. In 1852 at the Keighley Agricultural Show in Yorkshire, a weaver called Joseph Tuley was showing his Large White sows as well as some extra pigs. There was confusion amongst the judges about these other pigs, as they were too

small to be shown in the Large White class. 'The merits of these pigs were so extraordinary, entirely forbidding recourse to disqualification, a committee was summoned, whereupon the judges declared that, if removed from the Large White class the pigs would not be eligible for the Small White class'. The outcome of this event was the creation of a third class; the Middle White class. Thereby the new breed was recognised.

Chinese/Siamese characteristics

The Small White pig was cultivated for the show ring. It was a mix of the local Yorkshire pig and imported Siamese and Chinese pigs. The dished face of the Middle White, along with the characteristic pricked ears and short snout all originated from these Chinese and Siamese pigs. Unfortunately, the Small White became extinct in 1912.

Foundation stock for the National Pig Breeders' Association in 1884

The Middle White was extremely popular for its eating habits (they root less than other pigs), early maturing and extremely easy management so much so that when the National Pig Breeders' Association was launched in 1884, the Middle White, as well as the Large White and Tamworth, were established as the three foundation breeds, with their own herd books published that year.

The London Porker

The Middle White was regarded as a specialist pork producer in the first half of the twentieth century. It was extremely popular in London, where butchers cut carcasses into small joints and it was fondly known as 'the London Porker'. The breed has been widely exported. They are very popular in Japan where they are called 'Middle Yorks'.

Rationing

The Second World War bought a reversal of fortunes, as rationing (which carried on until 1954) led to a decline in pork breeds, which included, among others the Middle White. The concentration was now on pigs that produced quality bacon.

Popular Resurgence

As with many other breeds, it was because of the commitment of a handful of breeders that the Middle White has continued to this day. There is a resurgence of interest in the Middle White of late, with it being included on the menus of popular London restaurants. The celebrity chef Anthony Worrall Thompson is so enamoured with the breed that has even started to breed his own! He is the Patron of the Middle White Pig Breeders Club, which was founded in 1990.

Characteristics

As its name suggests, the Middle White pig is of medium size with sows weighing 200kg and boars 280kg. It is heavily built with a compact shape. The pig is hardy but requires refuge in acute temperatures. According to 2009 research, litters average at 8.99 piglets. The sows are maternal and the breed as a whole is known for its docility. Since they root less than other breeds they are more appropriate for some outdoor systems and will cause less damage to fencing.

Meat

The pig is an early maturing, specialist pork breed, being especially popular when killed at 3–4 months, when it has a live-weight of 65–70kg. The trouble with allowing it to get to a heavier weight is that meat contains too much fat. Piglets are another viable source of revenue, as suckling pigs reach 10–14kg liveweight. Another factor in the Middle White's success at market is its high killing out percentage. The killing out percentage is the dead-weight of an animal expressed as a percentage of its live weight. A very well-known example of this is a butcher in Chicago who achieved a killing out percentage with the Middle White of 90 per cent.

Vulnerable
(200 to 300)

Berkshire

- The Berkshire Pig is renowned as having the oldest pedigree of any pig in Britain.
- It was mentioned 300 years ago, by Oliver Cromwell's soldiers when they were deployed at Reading.
- Queen Victoria owned the first registered boar, named 'The Ace of Spades'.
- The American Berkshire Association was created in 1875 and will only register pigs that have been imported from recognised British herds, or those that can trace their lineage back to the original British imports.
- The modern Berkshire is completely black with the exception of white markings on the feet, nose and the tip of the tail.

Oliver Cromwell's Troops

The Berkshire pig, originating as its name suggests in the county of Berkshire, is renowned as having the oldest pedigree of any pig breed in Britain. It was mentioned 300 years ago, by Oliver Cromwell's soldiers when they were deployed at Reading; they talked about the size of the local breed and standard of its meat. The Berkshire at that time was a larger pig and had a great deal more colour variations that the pig that we know today.

Queen Victoria owned the first Registered Boar

During the Industrial Revolution in the late eighteenth and early nineteenth centuries, Asian pigs were used to improve the Berkshire. The breed was, and still is, very popular with the Royal Family. Queen Victoria owned the first registered boar, named 'The Ace of Spades' and even today, Windsor Castle is home to a sizable herd of Berkshires. Although having produced many champions in the latter nineteenth century, the Berkshire's popularity waned in the second half of the twentieth century as 'white' pigs and bacon production were necessitated.

Popularity in Japan

Today, the RBST keeps a herd at Aldenham Country Park in Hertfordshire as

well one at the South of England Rare Breeds Centre based in Kent. There are less than 100 purebred sows in Australia and New Zealand. The American Berkshire Association was created in 1875 and will only register pigs that have been imported from recognised British herds, or those that can trace their lineage back to the original British imports. The Berkshire is popular in Japan, where it is bred and trademarked under the name Kagoshima Kurobuta, or 'Kagoshima black pig'.

Black with White Points

Although originally found in a wide variety of colours, the modern Berkshire is completely black with the exception of white markings on the feet, nose and the tip of the tail. It is of medium size, with sows weighing about 220kg and boars 280kg. They are a solid breed with small legs, with a dished face and average length of snout. Their ears are carried erect and are edged with light hair. Shoulders are well sloping and their tail is set high. They have a straight underline, with a minimum of 12 teats. Berkshire pig meat is pinky, with heavy marbling. It is very tender and full of flavour. The pig matures early and should be reared for slaughter to 60–70kg in 3–4 months.

LARGE WHITE

- The Large White developed in the nineteenth century in Yorkshire.
- It became one of the founder breeds for the National Pig Breeders' Association, now known as the British Pig Association.
- The Howitt Report in 1955 chose the Large White, as well as the Welsh and the Landrace pigs, to form the fundamentals of pig production in the UK to increase food production after the Second World War.
- The Large White is now one of the most popular pig breeds in the world for cross-breeding in intensive pig farming. It has been exported to over 60 countries.
- It has an excellent feed conversion ratio and is able to maintain a superb daily live weight gain.

Founder Breed for the British Pig Association

The Large White developed in the nineteenth century in Yorkshire. It is hard to clarify which breeds the local, rough-boned, heavy, long-legged pigs were crossed with, although Davidson in *The Production and Marketing of Pigs* believes that they may have been crossed with the Leicestershire, Cumberland and Small and Middle White. The resulting Large White was favourably shown at the Windsor Royal Show in 1831. It became one of the founder breeds for the National Pig Breeders' Association, now known as the British Pig Association, and the first herd book was created in 1884. It is unusual in that it has not been crossed with Asian pigs, which was so popular in the late nineteenth and early twentieth century.

Chosen to Combat Rationing after the Second World War

By the end of the nineteenth century the Large White had made quite a name for itself and it was being widely exported across the world. Forward looking breeders with pure bloodlines were sending stock to Australia, Argentina, Canada, Russia and most of Europe, where it is commonly known as the 'Yorkshire pig'. The Howitt Report in 1955 chose the Large White, as well as the Welsh and the Landrace pigs, to form the fundamentals of commercial pig farming in the UK to increase food production after the Second World War. The Large White is now one of the most popular pig breeds in the world for cross-breeding in intensive pig farming. Both sows and terminal sires (that produce piglets for slaughter rather than breeding) are used widely creating a consistently high standard of progeny.

Alice Newth

World's Favourite Breed

In the 1970s the establishment of performance testing schemes created an international demand for pure Large White genetics. Between 1970 and 1972 over 8,500 Large Whites were sent overseas from the UK. Twenty years later, in the early 1990s, systems changed in the US, so that farmers were paid for the lean meat percentage rather than live-weight. This, the Large White excelled at and created another huge export market for these pigs from the UK. The Large White has been exported to over 60 countries, making it the world's favourite breed. However, due to excessive crossbreeding and hybridisation, the original Large White is becoming extremely rare.

Excellent Feed Conversion Ration and Daily Live Weight Gain

The Large White is hardy enough to cope with outdoor systems. As a cross, it is used more intensively. Its productivity is due to decades of performance recording and specialisation. Average litter size is 11–12 piglets per litter, with 2–3 litters per year. It has an excellent feed conversion ratio and is able to maintain a superb daily live weight gain. Boars range in weight from 350–380kg, whilst sows are 260–300kg. The pig is large, white and lean. It has characteristic erect ears and a dished face. It possesses good conformation with outstanding hams. A Large White will live for 9–15 years.

The expression 'sweating like a pig' is not derived from the animal. Pigs do not sweat profusely. They keep cool by wallowing in mud. The reference to 'pig' instead comes from smelting pig iron.

TAMWORTH

- Tamworths are believed to have direct lineage from the Old English Forest pig: the earliest native pig.
- Canada received their first Tamworths in 1888.
- Occasionally today, the Tamworth is crossed with wild boar, to create offspring that have meat with a unique gamey flavour.

Direct Lineage to the Earliest Native Pig

Long, lean, vigorous pigs were found in central England in the early nineteenth century. They were dark red in colour and were allowed to forage in the oak and beech woodlands throughout the colder months of the year. They were believed to have direct lineage from the Old English Forest pig: the earliest native pig. The Tamworth was not considered fashionable enough to improve by crossing it with Chinese and Neapolitan pigs in the late eighteenth century. However, in 1809, that all changed!

The Prime Minister Starts a Breed

Sir Robert Peel, Prime Minister of the United Kingdom between 1834–1835 and again in 1841–1846, travelled to Ireland and saw some pigs called 'Irish Grazers' which he subsequently imported to Drayton Manor, his estate in Tamworth, Staffordshire, crossing them with the local breed of pig. This had a knock-on effect in surrounding counties, such as Warwickshire, Leicestershire and Northamptonshire, where similar crossing also took place. By the mid-

Tamworth Breeders Club

1880s, uniformity had been achieved and the Tamworth was accepted as a breed by the Royal Agricultural Society in 1885, becoming part of the National Pig Breeders' Association of Great Britain.

Countryfolk Curing their Bacon

The herd book was started in 1885, but a few years earlier, in 1882, Thomas Bennett of Rossville, Illinois had begun importing the Tamworth pig into the United States. Canada received their first Tamworths in 1888. It is through exports and subsequent imports that genetic variability is maintained. Important populations of Tamworths are found today in the UK, US, Canada, Australia and New Zealand. They do well in more northerly areas such as Scotland and Canada, where they can cope with the wind and rain. They are particularly suited to forest grazing, enjoying bracken and using their long snouts to forage for their own food as they did in the past, when cottagers, as well as landowners, farmers and country folk would maintain pigs so that they could cure their own bacon. Their bristle protects them from the harmful rays of the sun, and when they moult, they seek shade, wallowing, which has the dual purpose of cooling them down as well as providing an effective sun block.

Distinctive Red Coat

Occasionally today, the Tamworth is crossed with wild boar, to create offspring that have meat with a unique gamey flavour. The pig typically thrives on

Michelle Baldock

low energy foods and is slow to mature, producing a lean, fine grained carcass, with up to a 70 per cent yield as their bones are so thin, giving a better meat to bone ratio without too much fat. The Tamworth is a medium sized pig, with an adult boar weighing 250–370kg and the female weighing 200–300kg. They tend to be in the region of 100–140cm long and 50–65cm high. Their curly tail is 24–30cm in length. They have long necks and legs, with deep sides and thin backs, with good, robust hams. They possess an elongated snout, slightly dished face and erect ears that are slightly inclined. Their most defining characteristic is their ginger, orange-red coat, which lends them the name 'Sandyback' or 'Tamworth Red'. Tamworths produce fewer piglets than commercial animals, with between 6–10 in a litter. The pigs are good natured and enjoy human interaction, although they can be defensive of their food if they share a pasture with other livestock.

Australian Imports Create a New Female Line

After the Second World War, numbers fell considerably so that by the 1970s there were just 17 boars alive. Canadian pigs were thought to be too dark a red, so Australian pigs were bought in. Boars from the Royal Standard, Golden Ranger and Glen lines were transported to the UK in 1976, and in the late 1990s both boars and gilts were imported to the UK, with boars incorporated into all the female lines, as well as the creation of a new female strain, 'Rita'.

BRITISH SADDLEBACK

- The British Saddleback is an amalgamation of two separate breeds: the Wessex and the Essex Saddlebacks.
- The Wessex pig came from the New Forest and was originally a mix of two native bygone English bacon pigs.
- During the Second World War, 47 per cent of all pedigree sow registrations were made up from the Essex and Wessex variety.
- The British Saddleback has found a following today in outdoor and organic markets.

The Essex

The British Saddleback is an amalgamation of two separate breeds: the Wessex and the Essex Saddlebacks.

The Essex was improved by Lord Weston, who whilst travelling in Italy, spotted some Neapolitan pigs that he liked the look of. He wanted to use them

ce Newth

to cross with his Essex sows and so bought a pair of Neapolitan boars and imported them back to his estate. One of his leaseholders, Fisher Hobbs who lived in Boxted Lodge, saw these Neapolitan-Essex boars that Lord Weston had created and used them to breed with his rough Essex sows, and in time instigated the new Improved Essex. He did so well, that in 1840 a boar and a sow, both propagated by Mr Hobbs, won first prize in their individual classes at the second Royal Agricultural Show, assembled in Cambridge.

The Essex, as its name suggests, had its stronghold in East Anglia. It had a black neck and head, with a precisely marked belt of white going over the shoulders and down over the forelegs. The remainder of colouration was black with occasional white feet and tail end.

The Wessex

The Wessex pig came from the New Forest and was originally a mix of two native bygone English bacon pigs. It proved popular, so that by 1914 it was found extensively throughout the South and South West. It shared similarities with the Essex in that it was black overall, with an unbroken belt of white over the shoulders stretching down to the forelegs.

The Wessex Saddleback Society, as explained by the writings of W.J. Walden, took strict measures to avert foreign blood being introduced, and they were delighted that there had been, unlike many other breeds, no contamination of the bloodlines by crossing with Chinese pigs. Walden rejoices in the amalgamation of the two breeds, seeing this as their distinguishing feature. He writes in 1931, 'Why then make a feature of the chief colouration marking? Surely it does not take a high intelligence to see the correctness and advantage of the one conspicuous trade mark when two China free breeds are bought together?'

The first individual herd books for both the Wessex and Essex breeds were created in 1918. The British Saddleback breed was not fully established until the printing of its own herd book, which occurred in 1967.

Dominance in Boar Licensing

Until then, both the Essex and the Wessex benefited from huge demand, particularly during the Second World War, at which time 47 per cent of all pedigree sow registrations were made up from the Essex and Wessex variety. Licensing in 1949 showed 2,435 Essex and Wessex boars being authorised, making up a huge 25 per cent of the overall sum. They continued to retain dominance by representing 22 per cent of the complete registrations in 1954. However, the white breeds, such as the Large White, Welsh and Landrace, were growing in popularity. 1954 also saw a drop in the licensing of Essex and Wessex boars, making up only 10 per cent of the total. In the post war rationing years, the advice given to pig breeders was to cross the Essex or Wessex sow with a white boar, creating a dual-purpose pig that consolidated both pork and bacon output.

Requirement of the Herd Book

To be eligible for the herd book the pig must be: bred in the UK or Republic of Ireland; have 12 sound teats; be ear-marked and recorded at birth with the British Pig Association; have parents already recorded in the herd book and be free from congenital defects. The pig must also meet many other specific requirements such as colour – the pig must be black and white, with a continuous belt of white hair stretching round the shoulders and forelegs, with white markings only on the nose, tip of tail and the hind legs, but no higher than the hock. Ears should be of medium size and curving, but not getting in the way of sight.

British Saddleback Today

The Saddleback has enjoyed popularity in Nigeria and the Seychelles, where it copes well with the heat and rough pasture. It is a hardy pig and does well in extensive farming. In 2009, on average 9.98 piglets were produced per litter. The sow is an excellent mother – the breed is known to be docile. British Saddlebacks are large, with distinctive lop ears and deep bodies. Disparities can occur in colouration, due to the fusion of the two different strains. Boars weigh 320kg, whilst the sow is about 270kg. Nowadays the pig is dual purpose, making a good pork, or bacon pig if allowed to grow to a heavier weight. It has found a following today in outdoor and organic markets.

GLOUCESTER OLD SPOTS

- There must be at least one spot on the pig's body for it to be accepted into the herd book and attain pedigree status.
- The pig historically was utilised in the cider and pear orchards of Gloucester.
- The Gloucester Old Spots is the first recorded pedigree pig and both the Prince of Wales and the Princess Royal keep them at their Gloucester properties.
- The application to the European Commission for Traditional Speciality Guaranteed status was afforded on 29 July 2010.

At Least One Spot!

The Gloucester Old Spots pig is named as its white body is endowed with black spots. There must be at least one spot on its body for it to be accepted into the herd book and attain pedigree status. The pig historically was utilised in the cider and pear orchards of Gloucester and would eat the windfall apples and pears as well as refuse from the local dairy farms. Local legend has it that the spots on the pig were created by bruises from dropping fruit.

Peasants and Princes

The breed society came into play in 1913. They named the breed Old Spots due to the fact that it had been around for time immemorial – long before anyone could remember. The initial pedigree documentation took place in 1885, which was long after similar records for horses, cattle and sheep, as pigs were considered a peasant's beast. However, the Gloucester Old Spots is the first recorded pedigree pig and both the Prince of Wales and the Princess Royal keep them at their Gloucester properties.

Carrier of Now Extinct Genes

Genetic input over the years seems to have come from the Lincolnshire Curly Coat and the Cumberland pig – both of which are now extinct, although there have been plans to recreate the latter. The Gloucester Old Spots has been used to develop the American Spot and Chester White pigs. They are valued for their docile temperaments and fantastic foraging abilities.

Traditional Specialty Guaranteed Status

With the onset of intensive farming and the requirement of mass production many British breeds were pushed aside, with falling numbers. However, magic can occur, and an application to the European Commission for Traditional Speciality Guaranteed status was afforded on 29 July 2010. This

TSG achievement asserts that the Gloucester Old Spots meat has particular qualities that are distinct from the remainder of pigs in its group, and that the pigs have been produced in the same way for at least 30 years. The Breed Society is dynamic in finding traders who mislead the public by selling meat as Gloucester Old Spots pedigree produce when it is in fact a cross-breed.

Cross-breeding to Feed the Western World

There have been several exportations over the years, but they have never experienced much success. Prior to the First World War, some Gloucester Old Spots were sent to America and were fundamental in creating the Spotted Poland China pig, now called the National Spotted breed. An exportation to Australia in the 1920s fizzled out ten years later. The 1950s saw a handful of pigs sent to the US where they were used to cultivate the Minnesota No.2 hybrid, which became the founder of the modern commercial cross that now provides the majority of pork and bacon to North America and Europe. Other exports to the US and Falkland Islands lost their pedigree status through cross-breeding. The Breed Society became anxious about losing their pig altogether if a catastrophic disaster like Foot and Mouth occurred.

A Viable, Pedigree Population Independent of the UK

It was not until 1995, when Robyn Metcalfe asked the society for help in creating a new breeding programme in the US that relief came. She asked for 20 unrelated pigs, which were carefully chosen by the society. The piglets had to go into isolation for a few months and received thorough veterinary tests. By the time they reached America they were nearly a year old, but they got there safe and sound, after endless paperwork, and a successful and appreciable population has been achieved. Robyn founded Gloucester Old Spots of America Inc., and the breed society in the UK could breathe a sigh of relief.

Marketing the Meat

Gloucester Old Spots meat is highly valued because of its fat content. It is higher than modern meat which show very little marbling inside the muscle. This fat warms the pig during its life outside, and it also bastes the meat in its own fat whilst it is cooking, giving a very mouth-watering, tender taste. To get the best flavour bacon it should be dry-cured. The Traditional Breeds Meat Marketing Company work with certified butchers all over the UK who will buy pedigree rare and traditional stock.

Qualifications and Disqualifications to the Breed Standard

The Gloucester Old Spot is broad, with a long, level back and a thick, deep body. Hams are large and full. Sows weigh in the region of 280kg whilst boars are 350kg. They have large, lop ears which drop forwards to the nose. Their face is marginally dished. The skin should be free of coarseness or wrinkles, and their hair must be silky and straight. There should be at least 14 well positioned teats. Disqualification from the breed standard, set by the British Pig Association, would include such characteristics as a blue undertone to the skin (unrelated to a spot), a sandy colouration on the skin, a heavy jowl or a furrow of bristles on the mane.

OXFORD SANDY AND BLACK

- The precise origin of the Oxfordshire Sandy and Black has been lost in the midst of time, but there are records of it dating back 200–300 years, making it one of Britain's oldest pigs.
- All that we can be certain of is that it evolved over 200 years ago in Oxfordshire, being a conventional farmer's or cottager's pig.
- Devoted breeders are gradually strengthening the tenuous lines.

One of Britain's Oldest Pigs

The precise origin of the Oxfordshire Sandy and Black has been lost in the midst of time, but there are records of it dating back 200–300 years, making it one of Britain's oldest pigs. It is thought to be connected to the old Berkshire and Tamworth pigs but not much is certain about their involvement – the Oxfordshire Sandy and Black could have evolved from them, or been a product of cross-breeding between them, or the result of a cross-breed with another pig – nobody really knows! All that we can be certain of is that they evolved 200 years ago

in Oxfordshire, being a conventional farmer's or cottager's pig. The Oxfordshire Sandy and Black is commonly called the Plum Pudding Pig, in reference to its markings, or the Oxford Forest Pig, showing the source of their origins.

Nearly Extinct – Not Once but Twice!

Nobody set up a breed society for the pig and it nearly became extinct, not once but twice in the twentieth century. Numbers fell as low as one or two boars being licenced a year in the 1940s. A handful of committed breeders kept the breed alive. When the Rare Breeds Survival Trust was formed in 1973 hope was raised, but the RBST did not acknowledge the Oxfordshire Sandy and Black and the breed continued to decline. It was not until 1985 that a breed society was formed and the breed at last had a management system behind it.

Strengthening the Tenuous Bloodlines

The breed society's first herd book recognised 29 herds, with 15 boars and 62 sows in total. Some bloodlines have died out since then, but devoted breeders are gradually strengthening the tenuous lines. The British Pig Association has subsequently taken over the herd book, with the advantages of heightened exposure and recognition at shows. There are now four boar and 13 sow bloodlines within the herdbook. Boar bloodlines are Alexander, Alistair, Clarence and Jack. Sow bloodlines are Alison, Clare, Clarissa, Cynthia, Dandy, Duchess, Elise, Gertrude, Gloria, Iris, Lady, Mary and Sibyl.

Natural Foraging Ability makes them Economical to Keep

The pigs have a wonderful temperament and mothering abilities. They do well in most systems but prefer an outdoor setting as they are instinctive foragers, making them very economical to keep. They finish more swiftly than other native breeds, and are less likely to run to fat. They are known for their pork, bacon and ham. They are a good-looking breed, with a sandy to rust colouration, including black patches on their coat. They have pale feet and lop ears with a slightly dished face.

WELSH PIG

- The Welsh pig pre-dates all records and has thus been around for centuries.
- The First World War saw a diminished supply of pork and bacon, with imports only allowed from Canada and the US. Pig farmers in Wales decided to set up their own breed society in order to expand provision.
- The Howitt Report of 1955 decided that three breeds, the Large White, the British Landrace and the Welsh Pig, were the most commercially viable pigs to rear.

Pigs of Yore

The Welsh pig pre-dates all records and has thus been around for centuries. The first we hear about the large, lop-eared white pig from Wales is in 1870 when there was a thriving trade in bringing Welsh and Shropshire pigs to Cheshire to fatten them up on dairy by-products.

First World War Imports

The First World War saw a diminished supply of pork and bacon, and imports were only allowed from Canada and the US. Pig farmers in Wales decided to set up their own breed society in order to expand provision. So, in South Wales in 1918, the Glamorgan Pig Society was established. This was followed on quickly by the Welsh Pig Society for West Wales, which was created in 1920. It was decided, after a series of discussions, that since the pigs in Pembrokeshire, Carmarthenshire and Cardiganshire were so similar, these breed societies would amalgamate to become the Welsh Pig Society in 1922, publishing their first herd book in 1924 and becoming part of the National Pig Breeders' Association (now the British Pig Association), in 1952.

Testing Pigs

Things took a turn for the better after the Second World War. The Howitt Report of 1955, written as a result of the rationing that the country had suffered, (which concluded on 4 July 1954), looked at how bacon and pork production

could be increased. They decided that three breeds, the Large White, the British Landrace and the Welsh Pig were the most commercially viable pigs to rear. They began a series of tests on the progeny of these pigs throughout the 1960s and 70s, with the Welsh catching up with the Large White and Landrace so that by 1974/75 the Pig Improvement Scheme Year Book reported that it had equal results in the testing programmes.

Rise and Fall

Of course, throughout this time, the Welsh pig was widely used commercially, with the total licences issued for Welsh boars rising from 41 in 1949 to 1,363 in 1954. Pedigree sow registrations increased from 880 in 1952 to 3,736 in 1954. However, the breed's success led to a sharp decline in the numbers of other native breeds. The Welsh pig began to suffer a drop in numbers from the 1980s, due to the increased popularity of hybrid pigs.

Nowadays, the breed is used to provide genetic material for farmers in cross-breeding initiatives. They are valuable due to their ease of care, their rapid live-weight gain at a low feed conversion ratio, providing a lean carcass, even at heavier weights, with a superlative killing out percentage. KO per cent indicates the weight of the carcass as opposed to the weight of the live pig immediately prior to slaughter. There are at present 14 boar lines and 32 sow lines.

Fourteen Teats

In 2009, the average litter size was 11.24. Sows have good mothering capabilities and both boars and sows should have a minimum of 14 teats. The pig has a long, pear-shaped body with its lop ears touching just before its straight nose. The legs are wide apart and it has well developed hams. Boars weigh in the region of 250kg, whilst sows are 150–200kg.

GOATS

VULNERABLE
(200 TO 300 BREEDING FEMALES)

Bagot

MINORITY
(500 TO 1000)

Golden Guernsey

BAGOT GOAT

- Bagot goats are thought to have come to Britain with the Knights of the Crusade during the Middle Ages.

- After the Second World War there was an extermination order placed on the entire herd, as they, along with the deer, were damaging crops.

- The Bagot goat has found work in conservation grazing, where they clear invasive woodland and shrub.

Ancestral Roots

The Bagot goat lived for six centuries as a single herd, semi-wild in the parkland of Blithfield Hall in Staffordshire. They lived there for 600 years in genetic isolation and were hunted like deer. They have appeared in historical documents since 1389, making them Britain's oldest recorded goat. The goats

Nick Bohemia and the Bagot Goat Society

are named after their keeper, Sir John Bagot.

The goats are thought to have come to Britain with the Knights of the Crusades during the Middle Ages and given to Lord Bagot by King Richard II of England in appreciation of fine hunting. The goat appears on the Bagot family's coat of arms, with two goats bordering a shield, which is topped by a goat's head. Sir John Bagot's helmet adorned with a goat's head, can be viewed today in Blithfield church.

European Relatives

The Valais Black-Necked goat of Switzerland shares similar characteristics with the Bagot goat. The Valais is an improved breed kept mainly for its meat. The Landrace breeds, found in Scandinavia, also have many properties in common with the Bagot goat. Although historically the Bagot is thought to have originated from the Valais goat, modern genetic analysis suggests that it is far more closely linked with the native British primitive goat.

Culling and Recovery

In 1710 there was intervention to cull the breed, as the goats were doing damage to nearby farmland. In 1938, the herd was again reduced as it had grown in number to more than 100. After the Second World War there was an extermination order placed on the entire herd, as they, along with the deer, were damaging crops. Lord Bagot defended his goats, which numbered 80 at the time, and a compromise was reached to limit the goats to 60. This level was kept until 1947, when numbers were allowed to rise once more. In 1954 numbers were up to 80 and some were sent to parkland in other areas of the country. In 1957 the 5th Lord Bagot sold the estate and the goats were scattered. Some probably went for dog meat. Nancy, Lady Bagot, bought 20 in 1962 and in time returned these to the Hall.

Striking Appearance

The Bagot goat is very striking in appearance. It is of small to medium size and possesses long horns that curve backwards with a sideways twist. The males have larger horns. The head and neck are jet black, with the rest of the body white. The colour change occurs around the shoulder line. They have long, shaggy hair with a white blaze above their eyes. They are splendid to look at.

Independent Air

They are feral animals and are therefore very cautious around humans. Even if domesticated, they still retain a nervy character. They are able to fend for themselves. Commercially, however, they have very few uses. They have not been cross-bred to improve their milk or meat and therefore numbers have dropped accordingly. Other goats, such as the Nubian and La Mancha are more useful for meat. The Alpine goat and the Toggenburg have high yields of milk, so are much more productive than the Bagot. The nervy character of the Bagot prevents it being useful for milking or being in harness. Although magnificent to look at, and the oldest recorded goat, they have very little agricultural use.

Finding a Purpose

The Bagot has, however, found work in conservation grazing, which suits their feral nature. They have a low maintenance diet and are put to work to clear invasive woodland, control thorny shrubs and brambles and clear shrub. Other breeders keep the Bagot goat for their good looks and unusualness. The RBST have classified the Bagot goat as Vulnerable, meaning that there are only 200–300 breeding females.

Minority
(500 to 1,000)

Golden Guernsey

- The Golden Guernsey can find its roots in the dolmens, or Megalithic graves that date back to 2000BC on the Channel Islands.
- Their recent ancestors are said to be the Syrian and Oberhasli goats.
- They are small in comparison to other goat breeds and fine boned.
- With the requirements of just a house and a small yard, their ability to stall feed, coupled with their incredibly affectionate, docile nature, this goat is an ideal house goat.

Megalithic Roots with Nazi Threat

The Golden Guernsey can find its roots in the dolmens, or Megalithic graves that date to 2000BC on the Channel Islands. Their recent ancestors are said to be the Syrian and Oberhasli goats. Modern records go back to 1826, when a guide book to Guernsey records a 'golden goat'. It was not until the 1930s that Dr Tracey, from the British Goat Society recognised the importance of these creatures and suggested to a Miss Miriam Milbourne that she re-establish the breed. She did just that, creating the L'Ancresse herd. She showed considerable bravery during the Second World War, when Germany troops eliminated most of the farm animals on the island. Miriam hid a fraction of her flock for a number of years, and in doing so kept the breed alive today. The Golden Guernsey was imported to mainland Britain in 1965 and the Goat Society Golden Guernsey register began in 1970. At the same time, Miriam's health began to suffer, and a trust was created to care for her stock, becoming the Golden Guernsey Goat Breed Society.

Small and Fine with a Golden Fleece

The breed is useful for free range or stall feeding, and is adaptable to the household, being friendly and very docile in temperament. They have erect ears, which are slightly upturned at the ends, with a straight or dished face allowed. There should be no tassels on the head. It is small in comparison to other goat breeds and fine boned. Its skin is gold, rather than grey or pink, and its wonderful coat can be a variety of shades of gold. Small white markings,

Church Farm Rare Breeds Centre

such as a blaze or star on the head are allowed, but no Swiss markings are permitted. These include light colours on the legs, tail or ears. The male tends to be hairier than the female.

Maiden Milkers – Perfect House Goat

With a moderate milk yield of 4–5 pints daily, the Golden Guernsey is an efficient producer given its comparatively small size and feed. Pasture fed nannies, when given some additional food, can produce this amount even when not in kid. They are thence termed 'Maiden Milkers'. Milk is high in butterfat (3.73 per cent) and protein (2.80 per cent) making it ideal for creating cheese or yoghurt. With the requirements of just a house and a small yard, its ability to stall feed, coupled with its incredibly affectionate, docile nature, this goat is an ideal house goat.

CHICKENS

A Priority Breed is represented by a *

Ancona	Minorca
Andalusian*	Modern Game*
Australorp	Modern Langshan*
British Araucana	Nankin
British Faverolles	Norfolk Grey
Brussbar*	North Holland Blue*
Buff and Non-Buff Orphington	Old English Game
Burmese*	Old English Pheasant Fowl*
Campine*	Rhodebar*
Cochin	Rosecomb
Cream Legbar	Rumpless Game*
Croad Langshan	Scots Dumpy*
Derbyshire Redcap*	Scots Grey*
Dorking*	Sebright
Hamburgh*	Sicilian Buttercup*
Indian Game	Spanish*
Ixworth	Sultan*
Legbar	Sussex*
Leghorn	Welbar*
Malay*	
Marsh Daisy*	

ANCONA

The Ancona chicken originated in the coastal town of Ancona, capital of the Marche region of Italy, where several native breeds, including the Leghorn, were combined. It was exported to England in 1851 where it was selectively bred to control the white colouration in its feathers. It found favour in the UK and US. Sadly numbers were very low in its indigenous Italy, where an enterprise in 2000 was launched, aimed at restoring the population and protecting diversity. It had once been the most widely distributed chicken in Italy.

The bird was introduced to the US from the UK in 1888. It comes in a rose-combed form and a single-combed variety. The first rose-combed birds were

RBST

exhibited in Birmingham in 1910. The American Poultry Association accepted the single-comb Ancona in 1898 and the rose-combed bird in 1914.

The Ancona chicken is a superb forager, with an active, bold disposition. It is a tough, resilient bird even in the coldest weather, but does not really like the heat. It tolerates confinement but tends to avoid contact with humans and takes flight readily. It is not particularly docile and is not broody. It will lay on average 220 large, white eggs a year, each weighing around 50g. Pullets start to lay at five months of age. Cocks weigh 2.5–2.8kg with a ring size of 18mm. Hens weigh 1.8–2.1kg with a ring size of 16mm. There are also Ancona bantams.

Ancona plumage is black, with white mottling. On average, one feather in every three shows a v-shaped white colouration at the tip. There are also white tips on the primaries, sickles and tail plumage. The black feathers have a beetle-green sheen. Italy accepts blue feathers in the chicken, but not the bantam. In Australia they standardise a red feathering as the ground colour. The Ancona chickens' legs are yellow, with black smudges. The beak is also yellow with black shading. The bird has orange-red eyes. Skin colour is yellow, and ear-lobes are white or cream.

ANDALUSIAN

The Andalusian chicken, as its name suggests, originated in the Andalusian region of Spain. Birds were imported to the UK from 1846 to 1851. From that date, there has been a long process of selective and cross-breeding of the birds to create the British Blue Andalusian that we know today. This is distinct from the Spanish bird which is known locally as the Gallina Andaluza Espanola, compared to the Gallina Andaluza Azul Britanica.

RBST

The only colour recognised in Britain is plumage of a blue-grey background colour with black hackles and lacing. Spanish birds exhibit a wider colouration and are known to be white with occasional blue-grey traces, white, gold partridge and silver partridge. However, the British blue is hard to breed because the blue colour is not a dominant gene, creating a 50 per cent success rate in the chicks. So, when two blue Andalusians are mated, half the chicks will show the same blue colouration, with a quarter showing black, and a quarter splash (predominantly white with indiscriminate blue-grey markings). However, all stock can be used to create new generations of Blue Andalusians since they all contain the same genes, whether dominant or recessive.

The birds lay approximately 160 large white eggs per annum, even during the winter months.

AUSTRALORP

The Australorp was devised from the Black Orpington bred in the UK by William Cook. Whilst the Orpingtons in the UK were being selectively bred as a highly-feathered exhibition bird, the Australians were trying their hand at egg production. Imported Orpingtons from the UK were crossed with the Rhode Island Red, as well as using the Minorca, White Leghorn and Langshan. The resulting birds were called Australian Black Orpingtons or Australorp.

It was in 1922–23 that things really took off. A trial of hens set a world record by laying 1,857 eggs throughout a 365-day period. With six hens, that averaged out at 309.5 eggs each a year. International excitement was ignited and orders were placed by the UK, US, Canada, Mexico and South Africa. In a later trial, one hen was recorded as laying 364 eggs in 365 days. A hen, looked after at home, can be expected to lay 250 light brown eggs per year, making the chicken one of the most favoured heritage utility breeds.

The Australorp also comes in a bantam size and are known to mature early, hens being ready to lay at five months. They come in three standard colours: black – with shimmering green feathering;

G. Walker

blue – darker lacing on slate coloured feathers; and white. Cocks weigh in the region of 3.9kg whilst hens are 2.9kg. Although renowned for their eggs, they make a good table bird and are friendly around children.

BRITISH ARAUCANA

The Araucana first arrived on British shores in the 1930s when a Chilean nitrate ship came into difficulty in the Inner Hebrides in Scotland. The bearded, muffed and tailed Araucanas that were on board were swept onto the beaches of these islands. The lineage of these birds went right back to the Arauca Indians of Old Northern Chile. When the Spanish invaded South America they brought with them light Mediterranean chickens, which they subsequently crossed with the Inca fowl. The Araucana Indians refused to be completely conquered by these Europeans and had the advantage of rocky and difficult terrain in the High Andes. Their chickens remained pure. Descendants of these chickens can still be seen in parts of the Amazon Basin and in the high altitudes of the Andes.

However, in the 1930s, having made their entrance on British shores, George Malcolm of East Lothian, Scotland developed the first modern standard, still used today. He kept the blue egg colouring and the crest, muff and beard. Strong-shelled, blue or green eggs are unique to the Araucana, in that the colour permeates throughout the whole shell. It is said that any chicken laying a blue egg will at some point have gathered Araucana genes. Araucanas will lay 250 eggs per year, even throughout winter.

George Malcolm went on to develop the bantam version in the 1940s, using Belgium bantams to cross. This initiated the lavender gene, which he then crossed into the Araucana chicken with great success and acclaim. The breed was standardised in 1960, and with the development of the Commonwealth, the British Tailed Araucana is now observed in more than 60 nations. The Poultry Club of Great Britain identifies 12 colours – black, black-red, blue, blue-red, crele, cuckoo, golden duckwing, lavender, pile, silver duckwing, spangled

Tim Martin Photography

and white. The birds are friendly, resistant to disease, and keen flyers, so their wings will need clipping.

BRITISH FAVEROLLES

The Faverolles initially came from the Eure and Loire region of France, to the west of Paris, where farmers would send eggs and chicken to the markets of the city. The little village of Faverolles is near the town of Houdan, which gives its name to another chicken.

As the city of Paris grew, and demand for meat and eggs increased, poultry was beginning to be imported from Asia, including Brahmas, Cochins and Langshans. They were mixed with the local birds, including the Faverolles, which was a proven egg layer, and subsequent birds became bigger, with a rapid growth rate. These crosses found great favour in Paris and soon the pure-bred Houdan was being left behind.

These Salmon Faverolles, known in France as 'tete de hibou' or 'the head of an owl', because of their distinctive beard and muff, were popular amongst farmers as they would both forage in woodlands or adapt to a battery cage. They were standardised in France in 1893. Again, the Houdan fell behind, as they did not like the battery cages and had to face the ultimate snub when the Houdan Club of France became the Houdan Faverolles Club de France in 1909.

Britain received its first Faverolles in the 1890s and it was so popular that by 1900 the British Faverolles Club was created with a new breed standard. Exhibition of birds was very important in the UK and a lot of money would change hands for the right bird. Breeders in France began to be more selective in order to meet these fulfilments. The Germans broke from the French and British as early as 1905 when they created a separate breed: the Deutscher Lachshühner.

Heath and Williams

The Faverolles produce 160–200 tinted eggs per year. The cock weighs 4.08–4.98kg, whilst the hen is 3.4–4.3kg. Standardized colours in the UK are black, laced blue, buff, cuckoo, ermine, salmon and white. They are a good meat bird, fast growing in contrast to other traditional breeds. Since the chicken is named after a village, it always has an 's' on the end of Faverolles, even when just talking about one chicken.

BRUSSBAR

The breed was generated by Professor Punnett and Mr Pease, working in Cambridge in the first decades of the twentieth century. They wanted to create an auto-sexing breed, where it is possible to differentiate between the sexes when the chicks hatch. They succeeded in this aim, with brown female chicks looking much darker than their male siblings. They did this by breeding Brown Sussex and Barred Rocks, the latter of which generated the different plumage in the chicks.

Professor Punnett and Mr Pease also

Nick Trotman

wanted to reproduce the characteristics of the Light Sussex, which was the most established breed of the moment. They bred in utility strains of this chicken to enhance efficiency.

They were successful in getting the breed standardised in 1952, but even though the auto-sexing characteristics were extremely valuable, the breed was never taken on as a commercial bird and so fell from popularity. It nearly became extinct, if it had not been for the efforts of one breeder near Bedford.

The Brussbar chicken is large and well built, with a phenotype close to that of a Sussex. It was developed to exhibit either gold or silver colouration. Nowadays the silver variety has died out. They have a characteristic 'crele' plumage with barring over a base colour combination of blonde and gold. They are good layers, and make a super table bird, but breeders these days are more worried about keeping this particular breed of chickens alive!

Buff and Non-Buff Orpington

The Orphington was developed in the 1880s by William Cook, and are named after his home town in Kent. William's father looked after horses at the inns along the busy London to Dover road. William worked with him for some time but decided to turn his attentions to chicken breeding. He found great fame and fortune in his pursuits, at a time when it was possible to earn a working man's annual wages for the same sum that a show champion might reach. The breeding of fowl was only just opening up and William took full advantage of this, writing extensively,

John Durrant

lecturing, acting as a consultant, selling appliances, feed and remedies, and producing the Poultry Keepers Account Book.

In 1880, Cook set about breeding a black chicken that he could exhibit in London, without showing the dirt and soot. He mixed Minorcas, Langshans and Plymouth Rocks to get the desired results. It was in 1886 that these black hybrids were exhibited at three big shows: Dairy, Crystal Palace and Birmingham, with a new club, the Orpington Club being created in 1887. Subsequently, in 1888, these Black Orpingtons were given their own classification at the Dairy Show in Islington.

There was a desire in the public for buff coloured birds, so Cook began developing the Buff Orpington in 1886. It was first shown at the Dairy Show in 1894. The public loved it and it gained huge popularity for a good few years as the favoured exhibition and heavy utility breed. Cook wanted them to be a dual-purpose bird, but due to the frenzy of activity on the poultry show scene, where large amounts of money were to be made, Cook decided, as he had done with the Black Orpington, to increase the feathering, which meant their meat and egg functions were compromised. The Buff Orpington Club was formed in 1898.

The Poultry Club of Great Britain requires a weight of 3.60–4.55kg for a male and 2.70–3.60 for a hen. They have a big, heavy body, with lots of feathering which is also found on the legs, and a small, curvy back. They come in a bantam size. Strains vary, but you can expect 90–175 light brown eggs in a year. They are very friendly chickens and can be handled, but tend to get bullied by other chickens, so require a lot of space. They don't like wet conditions or extreme heat. They make the ideal first chicken and family pet!

BURMESE

The emergence of the Burmese bantam in the UK dates back to around 1880 when a British army officer stationed in Burma (now Myanmar) sent a trio of birds to an associate officer in Scotland. Unfortunately, the two hens died, but the cock remained and was sent onto W.F. Entwisle, a renowned bantam breeder. He selectively bred it with his prototype Sultan bantams, being careful to breed only with offspring that matched the original cockerel.

However, his work was to be in vain and by 1914 the birds were considered extinct. It was not until around 1970 that a certain Andrew Sheppy was gifted some, believed to be the only survivors from the earlier stock. Andrew began to selectively breed them again, using White Booted bantams.

He succeeded and today we have the Burmese bantams, albeit rare. Both sexes are white with short feathered legs and a feathered crest with a single comb. The RBST and the Rare Poultry Society

Jed Dwight

encourage breeders to conform to the single crests and to look to the century old J.W. Ludlow and Harrison Weir drawings for standard shape, carriage and style.

The Burmese bantam requires housing and should be kept away from mud. Mown grass is more suitable for their dense white plumage and feathering on their feet. They are modest layers and the Society is keen for breeders to incubate these eggs rather than eat them.

CAMPINE

dwin and Mannion

Campines were imported to the UK in 1897, with the UK Campine Club formed in 1900. They came from the Campine region in the north-east of Belgium, just south-east of the Netherlands. There is also a very similar type of chicken in Belgium called the Braekel, which is found in the market town of Brakel, just west of Brussels. The birds here are heavier than the Campine, as the land is of a fertile, agricultural quality compared to the forested, less rich land in Campine. Although initially considered in Belgium to be two distinct breeds, they were combined under a single standard in 1925. The Campine in the UK, comes in two varieties; silver and gold, with both sexes exhibiting the same pencil feathering. The silver bird has a completely white head and neck hackles, and the remainder of the bird is barred with beetle-green feathering on a white background. The gold variety shows the same patterning, but the head and neck hackles, along with the background colour of the body, are gold.

The birds are incorporated by the RBST as a UK native breed because of the hen feathered males selected by British breeders. Belgian enthusiasts had always killed the hen feathered males, thinking them abnormal, but J. Wilson of Penrith began breeding these males that he procured from some Belgian eggs. He exhibited his first hen feathered cockerel in 1904 and from this one bird a whole breed was created. It was embraced as the standard Campine in the UK and numerous other countries.

The hens lay approximately 180 medium white eggs every year, although exhibition birds may produce quite a lot less. The birds are great at free ranging, being curious and animated. However, they can be skittish and infrequently go broody. The Campine Club was absorbed by The Rare Poultry Society in 1969.

COCHIN

The Cochin chicken came to the UK in 1843 from what is now Vietnam, but at the time was a French colony named Cochin-China. The birds were large with feathered feet, but in that era, any large bird from East Asia was termed a Cochin. The birds we know today are not closely related to these original imports, although they share the same name. It was not until 1847 when chickens imported from Shanghai saw a sudden surge in interest, known as 'hen fever', that gripped the Western world. They were the ancestors of our modern-day Cochin.

These birds were selectively bred to create the six standardised colours acceptable in the UK of black, blue, buff, cuckoo, partridge and grouse and white. There are no recognised Cochin bantams in the UK. They are known separately as Pekin bantams, originating from Pekin,

Alicia S

a very different area. This naming was the subject of much speculation, as in the rest of the world, Cochin bantams are almost indistinguishable from the UK's Pekin bantam.

The Cochin chicken has extravagant plumage which extends to the legs and feet. White Cochins are known to be easier to breed than getting the exact shading of buff or partridge, but, similarly to other white chickens, they do require shade to prevent their feathers becoming yellowy-copper (brassy) in the sun. Food such as corn, grass, leafy greens and marigolds can also cause brassiness. Mud should be avoided because of the feathering on the feet.

The hen will lay 150–200 small, tinted eggs per year. The cock weighs 4.5–5.1kg, whilst the hen is 4.1–5kg. They are docile, friendly birds and make wonderful pets, although they do need large quantities of food and take a long time to grow into the large, flocculent feathered birds that were, in the past, used to fill pillows and mattresses.

CREAM LEGBAR

RBST

The Cream Legbar was created at the Genetic Institute in Cambridge by Professor Reginald Crundall Punnett and Michael Pease. They had already successfully bred the Cambar in 1929, which was their first auto-sexing chicken: a mixture of the Barred Plymouth Rock and the Gold Campine. Their second venture was intended to create another auto-sexing breed with the purpose of egg production. They blended the Barred Plymouth Rock (which contained the auto-sexing gene) with the Brown Leghorn to create the Gold Legbar. This was standardised in 1945. Later, this was mixed with the White Leghorn to create a cream bird, which was further bred with the blue-egg laying Cream Araucana, which brought about the crest and the blue colour of the eggs.

The birds lay in the region of 180–200 blue, green or olive coloured eggs each year. As an auto-sexing breed, it is possible to distinguish the male chicks from the females when they are just a day old. Females possess light and dark stripes on their plumage whereas males are paler with a definite yellow spot on their head. The birds are willowy and refined. They were standardised in 1958 but reached a low in the 1970s as there was not a market for blue eggs. Since then, the breed has picked up again, thanks to the Wernless Collection and David Applegarth.

CROAD LANGSHAN

The Croad Langshan has a long history, originating from the Langshan region of China, near Shanghai, where chickens have been domesticated for 7,000–

Croad Langshan Breed Society

8,000 years. It is commonly believed that Major F.T. Croad was the first to import the bird to the UK in 1872. There was some controversy to begin with as the bird showed many similarities to the black Cochin, but this was resolved and in 1884 the Langshan Society was created. Major Croad's niece, Miss A.C. Croad was a keen supporter, but disagreed with the decision made at the AGM in 1887 to selectively breed for tight feathering, in essence moving away from the utility fowl to a show breed – the Modern Langshan. She left the Society around 1890 and by 1904 she was ready to form the separate Croad Langshan Club.

Cocks can stand 90 cm tall. The birds have a long, deep breast that sits well forwards. The tail rises sharply, creating a characteristic U-shape between the head and the tail. The majority of the chickens are black, with a beetle green tinge, but occasionally you will see a white bird. The shanks and outer toes are feathered. The legs are slate grey, but the soles of the foot should be pink. Hens will lay around 150 eggs a year, which are buff with a plum-coloured bloom. They were the first Asian chickens to produce brown eggs in the UK - rare until that time. Cocks weigh 4.3kg and hens 3.4kg. There is a bantam version.

It is difficult to breed Croad Langshans, due to the lack of genetic variation. Inbreeding can cause many problems, such as low fertility, reduced size and bone abnormalities. However, there is renewed interest in the breed in Australia, which will hopefully enlarge the genetic pool. They have been used in the development of Australian Langshans, Australorps and Orpingtons amongst others.

DERBYSHIRE REDCAP

The bird originally came from Derbyshire and the Pennines. It was first documented in the early nineteenth century and is thought to have been developed from the Golden Spangled Hamburg, Old English Pheasant

Fowl and Dorking. It is very alike in configuration to Yorkshire Pheasant and Lancashire Moonie, both of which are now sadly extinct.

This chicken is famed for its enormous rose comb seen in the cockerels once they reach three years of age. The British breed standard requires the comb to be greater than 7cm long with little fleshy points and a prominent spike which hangs backwards, known as the 'leader'. The biggest combs seen in cocks are in the region of 8.5cm x 7cm.

They are light fowl, with the male weighing 3.4kg and the female 2.75kg. Combs, wattles and earlobes should be vivid red. Plumage is a range of red, brown and black, with cocks showing a wider variety of colouration. Both sexes have black tails and black semi-circles on the margin of their body feathers. Beaks are a horn colour, with legs and feet being slate.

The birds are dual purpose, with the hens laying 150–200 large white eggs annually. The hens rarely go broody. The meat is said to be gamey. They have never been used commercially but being good foragers they like free range conditions and are the perfect farmyard chicken, even doing well in very cold conditions. They declined in popularity after about 1945, and by 1960 they were extremely scarce. In the US, the Derbyshire Redcap was registered on the American Poultry Association's Standard of Perfection in 1888, but they are now regarded as Critical by the American Livestock Breeds Conservancy.

DORKING

The Dorking was first documented in 47AD by a Roman writer who comments on the extra fifth toe that the birds possess. It is unclear whether the Romans bought them over from Italy, or whether they found them here. The fifth toe appears to have no useful function, although it is a key breed characteristic. The chickens are named after the market town of Dorking, in Surrey, where for hundreds of years they were transported to markets in London. It was not until the early twentieth century that the Sussex chicken ousted the Dorking in this respect.

The Dorking was among the birds included for exhibition at the first Poultry Show at London Zoo in 1845, and was featured in the initial poultry standard; The Standard of Excellence in Exhibition Poultry, published in 1865. Their popularity not only as an exhibition bird, but also for the table, continued right up to the First World War, with several breed societies being formed. At the end of the war the breed bordered on extinction, with farmers choosing faster growing hybrid chickens, until, in 1970, the Dorking Club was reformed.

Sharon Smith

The Dorking has traditionally been used for meat, although hens lay 120–170 large creamy white eggs per year. The cock weighs 4.55–6.35kg, and the hen 3.6–4.55kg. The Dorking also comes in a bantam form. There are five colourways: dark, white, cuckoo, silver grey and red. Silver grey is the most common plumage colour, whilst white is the hardest to find. The Silver grey hen exhibits silver grey plumage with darker grey pencilling. The comb on the male may freeze in cold weather.

HAMBURGH

The Hamburgh, in the UK and Australia, is also known as the Hollands hoen in the Netherlands and the Hamburger in Germany. The breed assimilated from two different strains. One of these was the Pencilled Hamburgh that came over from the continent and the second strain was from a number of breeders in Lancashire, Derbyshire and Yorkshire who selectively bred the Bolton Grey, Lancashire Mooney and Yorkshire Pheasant. These chickens were shown competitively in pubs across Yorkshire and Lancashire long before the first poultry show held at London Zoo in 1845. This poultry show led to the emergence of breed standards and further poultry exhibitions. In the north, people became despondent about their own local standards grouping these birds together under the Derbyshire Redcap and the Hamburgh breeds.

The Hamburgh gained a lot of prestige through exhibiting at shows, leading to the creation of the British Hamburgh club in the 1890s, as well as regional clubs in Scotland and Wales. However, the First World War took its toll, and numbers were severely depleted, never to be salvaged. They have only managed to cling on to existence in the UK due to the valiant efforts of a few breeders.

Cocks weigh around 2.25kg, hens are 1.80kg. They are also available as bantams. Germany and Holland describe 11 separate colour markings, including black, silver pencilled, gold pencilled, silver spangled and gold spangled. They need space to forage and scratch and are known to be

Terry Mayna

hard to breed, although they do produce 150 white eggs each year. They are typically feisty and excitable so are not necessarily a good bird to have around young children. They are not known for their meat and apart from their eggs, their main function is as an exhibition or ornamental bird.

INDIAN GAME

The Indian Game evolved in Cornwall and Devon by crossing the local Cornish chickens with imports from Asia, such as the Asil and Malay, which came into the docks of Falmouth and Plymouth. These birds were initially raised for fighting, being heavy, muscular birds, but cockfighting became illegal in England in 1849. They gained favour as a table bird and the Indian Game Club was created in 1886, having been exhibited at the Crystal Palace Shows of 1858 and 1859. The bird was improved further to have even stubbier legs and a wider body. This became a problem for male birds as they were unable to mate due to their short stature. Breeders got around this problem by mating their longer-legged cocks with their finest hens.

Hens will produce 100 tinted eggs a year, but due to their broad breast, they make an excellent bird for the table. They are frequently used to improve meat production in other chickens and have been referred to as the 'bulldog amongst chickens'. The bird was recognised by the American Poultry Association in

1893, who renamed it in 1905 to the Cornish Indian Game. It was renamed Cornish in the USA in 1910, as the use of the term 'Game' became unpopular. It is now used extensively to create hybrid broiler chickens all over the world.

The birds come in three colours – dark, jubilee and double laced blue. Dark is the most prevalent and was the original colour. Double laced blue is very hard to find. The birds have close feathering with no fuzz. They are hardy but can suffer in cold weather, as their tight feathering does not protect them. They are not flighty and are easily contained but do need low perches as they develop slowly.

RBST

IXWORTH

The Ixworth chicken was developed by Reginald Appleyard, beginning in 1931, and was first introduced at the 1938 London Dairy Show. The chicken was named after the village in Suffolk where he was born. Reginald Appleyard also created the Silver Appleyard Duck. With the Ixworth, he intended to create a dual-purpose chicken that would be a fast growing, top quality meat bird with proficient egg-laying quantities. He used a mixture of the White Sussex, White Minorca, White Orpington, White Old English Game and the Dark Indian Game in its make-up. Rapid developing hybrid broilers brought the Ixworth dangerously close to extinction in the 1950s, but rare breed safeguarders kept the breed alive. Today, it

RBST

is thought there are 20 or so keen breeders.

The Ixworth is a medium to large chicken, with a large body, white legs that have a pink hue, orange eyes and red comb. There is only one colourway – white. Their meat is said to be the finest of any pure breed. Like most pure breeds, they are best eaten before 12-14 months old. You can expect 150–180 medium sized, creamy white eggs per annum. There was a bantam version of this chicken, created in the 1950s, but it died out within ten years. Some breeders prefer a smaller chicken with a more exciting plumage. However, research at the Roslin Institute discovered that an Ixworth hen would attain a live weigh of 4.03kg at 55 weeks, with a mean of 0.74 eggs daily, which had a weight of 63.6g each. Being energetic foragers, they need a free range, although they are placid. Their meat obtains first rate prices.

LEGBAR

Professor Punnett continued his work creating auto-sexing chickens after the success of the Cambar, which was bred in 1929 at the Genetic Institute in Cambridge, using a Barred Plymouth Rock and Gold Campine. He worked with Mr M. Pease with the aim of selectively breeding a chicken with auto-

ck Trotman

sexing qualities as well as good egg laying abilities. They used the well-known layers, the Leghorn, and again the Barred Plymouth Rock, which had the sex-associated barring gene. They were successful in using the Brown Leghorn in this cross, creating the Gold Legbar, which became standardised in 1945. Using the new Gold Legbar and crossing it with a White Leghorn and Silver Cambar gave the Silver Legbar, which was standardised in 1951. The Cream Legbar was standardised in 1958. The Poultry Club of Great Britain considers the Cream to be a type of Legbar, however many think of it as a separate breed, as it is so different from the Gold and Silver Legbar. It is dealt separately in this book (see above).

The breed was broadly exported. However, they never caught on commercially as early layer hybrids were chosen instead. Gold Legbars are now considered rare in the UK, whilst the Silver is thought to be non-existent. They can be newly created by breeding Gold Legbars with Silver Duckwing Leghorns, and the Silver colouration would have to be selected for quite a few generations. The Gold Legbar cock has a grey barred plumage on its chest, legs and tail, with a gold and blonde barred neck and saddle. The hen will have similar grey and brown barring on its back and wings, with a salmon colouration on her breast. She will lay around 180 white/cream eggs per year. Female chicks hatch with prominent dark and light stripes over their body, whilst males are paler with a yellow patch on their head. Breeders are therefore able to remove the males that they do not want.

LEGHORN

The Leghorn originates from the countryside of Tuscany in Italy. It takes its name from the port town of Livorno, from which it was initially exported to North America. The date of this preliminary export is not exactly known, with different dates given, from 1828 to 'about 1830' and 1852. They were first called 'Italians' by their new North American breeders, and it was not until 1865 in Worcester, Massachusetts that they began to be called Leghorns.

The bird was imported from the US into the UK in 1870 and from here, back to Italy. The UK and the US started shipping different colour variations back and forth across the Atlantic, but they were ultimately after different things, and the exports stopped after the First World War. In the UK, it became fashionable to have larger combs and more sizable birds, whilst the Americans preferred a smaller size, with little combs. Even today, British and North American Leghorns can be easily distinguished.

The Americans used the bird prolifically as a battery hen, as the Leghorn is a great producer of white eggs, averaging 280 a year, but sometimes reaching 300–320. They are not good table birds. They come in a wide variety of colours standardised in the UK, ranging from black, blue, buff, cuckoo, golden

I. and C. M

duckwing, silver duckwing, exchequer, black mottled, red mottled, partridge, pile and white. Cocks weigh 3.4kg, whilst hens are 2.5kg. They don't often go broody and can fly well.

MALAY

The Malay chicken was bought to the UK around 1830 from the Orient, where it was commonly found across north India, Malaysia and Indonesia. It is related to the ancient Asil chicken of India, which has a 3,500-year history, although it is difficult to ascertain which breed was catalogued first. It was selectively bred throughout the UK, but particularly in Devon and Cornwall, as the boats from the East India Company arrived in Falmouth. By 1834, Germany and Holland had received their first imports of the Malay, and by 1846, the Malay had made its way to the US. It was exhibited at the first British poultry show in 1845 and made the first edition of the British Poultry Standards of 1865 where the black/red and white colourations were formalised.

M. Stephenson

The Malay is the tallest chicken breed, often standing a metre high with a long erect neck and lengthy strong legs. The head, neck and tail form three curves on their upright body, which is held proudly with a deep chest, although their comparative height can make them look a little scrawny. Their skull is large, with an expression that has often been described as 'cruel'. They have been selectively bred to increase egg production, which is now at 70–120 eggs a year compared to the 30–55 eggs expected annually in the 1970s.

A bantam form was introduced at the turn of the twentieth century. Again, these are relatively large, and although popular for a time, like the Malay chicken, they are also rare. In Asia the birds' purpose was for cock-fighting. At present, in the UK, they are used for exhibition and ornamental reasons, although this is not a bird to be kept as a family pet. Males will fight each other, although generally not as violently as other Asian game fowl. Their bad temper increases with confinement and they need space to roam. Opinion on their meat is polarised, with some saying it is too dry whilst others complimenting the quantity found on each bird.

MARSH DAISY

The Marsh Daisy was created by John Wright of Marshside, Southport, Lancashire in 1880 by crossing an Old English Game Bantam x Cinnamon Malay cock with Black Hamburgh x White Leghorn hens. Mr Wignell and Charles Moore suggested the addition of Sicilian Buttercups. The name for the bird is thought to derive from the similarity of its big red comb which looks like the Marsh Daisy flower (*Armeria maritima*) which grows in the marshy areas of Lancashire.

A breed club was first formed in 1913, but the bird was not exhibited until 1920. It was popular amongst small holders as a dual-purpose bird but never attracted interest for exhibition or commercial use. By 1940 its numbers were beginning to fall. It did not find favour overseas. Although the hens lay well – 250 tinted eggs per annum, and continue to do so for 3–4 years, the egg size

Dawn Teverson

is small. Fertility has fallen over the last few decades and a hatching of 50 per cent is reasoned to be satisfactory, although some breeders report more. A small gene pool does not help matters.. Hens do not often go broody. The Marsh Daisy also takes it time to mature, and is a lightweight breed, with cocks reaching 2.95kg and hens 2.5kg. This breed has no bantams.

Present day breeders are trying to stabilise the three main colours found in the birds: brown, buff and wheaten. This development was not fully completed in the 1920s and 30s. Other, much rarer colours are black and white. They all have distinctive rose combs (which lie flat on the head, embedded with circular lumps), white earlobes and willow green legs. The birds love to forage and need to be kept free range. They are docile and easy to keep, mixing well with other chickens.

MINORCA

The Minorca is, as its name suggests, indigenous to the Spanish island of Minorca, part of the Balearic Islands to the south-east of Spain. Some say the birds arrived in Spain with the Moors from Africa, and they are indeed referred to as 'Moorish fowl' in literary history. Others believe the birds came with the Romans.

They arrived in England with Spanish prisoners of war, when a merchant

ship was apprehended during the Colonial Wars in 1781. They were known in Britain as the 'Red Faced Spanish'. It is thought that these birds were really Castilian chickens, which were the fore-bearers of the Minorca.

They proved incredibly popular, not just for their egg laying abilities – they could lay 180–200 very large white eggs per year – but also for exhibition. By 1900 there were ten breed clubs in operation. However, breeders wanted to improve their performance in the show ring. They selectively bred to amplify their size, by crossing with Langshans and Orpingtons, and focused on increasing comb and lobe faculties, to the detriment of other qualities, notably utility. The Minorca is the heaviest light breed in the UK.

The bird is usually seen in black. Blue and

John Harrop

white varieties are rare, especially in the bantam. The male's comb stands up straight, whereas it falls to one side in the female – referred to as a folded comb. Cocks weigh 3.2–3.6kg, whilst hens are 2.7–3.2kg. They are active foragers and require free range conditions. The Minorca seems free of the usual poultry diseases. Young birds require a two metre fence, but they are not generally considered to be fliers. They rarely go broody.

MODERN GAME

The Modern Game is derived from the fighting cocks of the nineteenth century. With the abolition of cock fighting in 1849, many breeders turned to the show ring. By around 1870 the bird became known as the 'Exhibition Game', and the 'Modern Game' and was selectively bred by 1890. They were extremely popular and by the turn of the twentieth century, birds could fetch up to £100, which in todays' money equates to £1,000s. The main breeders were well-off people who could afford to employ chicken managers to look after their birds. In the 1920s, popularity fell, in part because these breeders would not let go of any of their good birds. The two World Wars saw the reduction in numbers of the Modern Game and it never regained its prevalence. The bantam version, however, has always been, and continues to be, extremely popular.

RBST

The bird has an upright stance, short back, tapering tail, extremely long legs and hard feathering. It has a very small comb and wattles. It comes in 15 colour variations: red faced (black-red/partridge, black-red/wheaten); pile; duckwing (blue, gold and silver); blue-red, white and crele; and the dark or mulberry faced (birchen, brown-red, black, blue, silver-blue and lemon-blue). It is not known as a table bird and is a poor layer, with 90 or so small eggs a year, subject to the strain, although the hens do go broody and make wonderful mothers. Its main purpose is as an exhibition bird. However, they make great pets as they are friendly towards people and are easily tamed.

MODERN LANGSHAN

RBST

The Langshan was first imported from northern China by Major F.T. Croad in 1872. This caused a stir as specialists thought they were similar to Black Shanghais, which were a less fluffy version of the later Black Cochins. The Langshan Society was set up in 1884, with members at the turn of the century wanting to create a more tightly feathered bird with longer legs and a higher carriage to set them apart from the Black Cochin. Miss A.C. Croad, niece of the Major, did not appreciate this move, and left the society in 1890s, creating her own Croad Langshan Club in 1904.

The Langshan Society carried on until 1939, but the Second World War saw a suspension of activities. The Society never re-established. The son of the last secretary kept a flock going until 1970 and he then gave them to preservers of rare poultry. There is thought to be only one flock surviving. Although in China, the birds are used for meat and eggs, the breed has undergone such development in the UK that it is classed as a native rare breed. It is now used, in the UK, for neither meat or eggs.

It is a tall bird, with tight feathering, and although they look slim, the cocks actually weigh 4.55kg. They are usually seen in black, but also come in blue or white. They are docile birds and can be very broody. They can be kept in runs, but their tall size should be reflected in the choice of housing.

NANKIN BANTAM

The Nankin is one of Britain's oldest bantams. It originates in south-east Asia and was widespread in the UK in the eighteenth century, although there is evidence of their existence in Britain dating back to the sixteenth century. Sir John Sebright, working in 1780, used the Nankin to create his Gold Sebright bantam. The Buff Orpington and Plymouth Rock bantams also use Nankin genes in their development. During the nineteenth century there were no

P.M. Fieldhouse

reports of Nankin bantams in south-east Asia by colonial powers, so it was thought that the UK was primary home to the breed. The 1850s saw the advent of poultry shows, and more exciting foreign birds got the most attention. There are only a handful of records of the Nankin in show results. By the early 1900s interest had dwindled to just three surviving breeders – Mr Cresswell, Mrs Ricketts and Mrs Cross. The Martin family, from Wisbech, began to keep them, and in 1955 Mrs Peters, in Sussex, bought some and began their renaissance. Over the years, some of the jaunty style and petite size has been lost. Since the 1980s there has been increased interest in the Nankin along with an attempt to recreate them in the style of the photographs in the 1921 *Encyclopaedia of Poultry* by J.S. Hicks taken of Mrs Cross's birds.

There is no chicken equivalent to the Nankin bantam. It comes in two variants: single comb and rose comb and there is just one colourway. Females have buff feathers with bronze or black markings on their tails, while males are notably more golden with longer sickle feathers. Beaks are a light horn colouration and legs are slate blue. Wings are large and downward slanting, which enables them to fly, although they are not flighty birds as a rule. As a slow maturing bird, they are not valued for their meat, and will lay 120–140 small, tinted eggs a year. They are good broodies and make excellent mothers. Indeed, along with other bantam breeds, broody Nankin hens were customarily employed to incubate game bird eggs such as partridge, quail and pheasant. If it were not for this capability, the Nankin may have become extinct.

The breed entered the American Poultry Association's Standard of Perfection in 2012, after the initial breed club was created in 2006. The name, 'Nankin' is said to have derived from the Chinese nankeen cloth, which was widely used in the nineteenth century (for example in the manufacture of gentlemen's trousers), and is a similar colour to the female's plumage.

NORFOLK GREY

I.P. Simpson

This bird was first cultivated by Fred Myhill of Hethel, Wymondam, Norfolk, around 1910–1912, as a dual purpose, meat and egg, utility bird. It is not known what birds were used in its make-up, but it is thought to be mostly Silver Birchen Game, which gives its meat a delicious flavour, and the Duckwing Leghorn, which increases egg production.

Fred Myhill went off to serve in the First World War and his birds were permitted to run freely in his absence, breeding with other birds in the process. When Fred came home he saw all his efforts had been dismantled. Needless to say, he started again, and by 1920 he took some of his chickens to the Dairy Show. They were presented under the name of Black Marias, which was the common name for a German military shell at the time. This name, however, was not popular, so that by 1925 Fred Myhill made an application to the Poultry Club of Great Britain, changing the name to Norfolk Grey. Immediately there was some success with this, gaining the attention of a number of new breeders, and the Norfolk Grey Club was formed.

Fortune was not on the Norfolk Grey's side. Its popularity fell, and by 1960 they were believed to be extinct. However, the Reverend Andrew Bowden and his wife Sue spotted some Norfolk Greys at a farm near Banbury and bought the birds, ensuring their survival.

There is only one colourway with the Norfolk Grey and that is black with silver white hackles. The cock has more silver hackles than the hen. The hen rarely goes broody and produces 230 medium sized, light brown/tinted eggs a year. They are known as a good table bird, with the cock reaching 3.2–3.6kg and the hen 2.25–2.7kg. They are hardy and not prone to usual poultry problems and like to forage in a free-range set-up.

NORTH HOLLAND BLUE

The North Holland Blue originates from the Noord Hollandse Hoender from the Netherlands. The bird was created around 1900 to fulfil the demand for white chicken meat in Amsterdam. The Belgian Maline chickens had been

brought in to supply the city, but they did not like the poor environment of north Holland, so they were crossed with hardy local chicken to create the heavy meat breed needed for the city. Some of these birds were imported to the UK where they were heavily used in the UK's chicken industry from 1934 to 1960, until they were supplanted by American hybrid chickens. The last farm closed in 1977, and since then they have been in rapid decline, being kept alive by the sole efforts of Les Miles, who kept a flock in his small back garden in Enfield. He died in 1992, aged 92, having made a real difference to poultry conservation.

The breed was standardised in the UK as having feathered legs, although the Dutch version has clean legs. They are auto-sexing, which means you can tell the genders apart at hatching, with the males being lighter in colour than their sisters. Only 20 per cent of chicks are hard to sex, but as adults, the male continues to be lighter. They are good table birds with the cock weighing 3.8–4.8kg. Hens will lay 150–180 largish, light brown eggs per annum. They come in only one colour – cuckoo, but their name derives from the fact that they look blue from a distance. They are docile and easy to manage.

OLD ENGLISH GAME

Records of Julius Caesar show evidence of the forefathers of the Old English Game bird in Britain in the first century BC. Their primary use was in cock-fighting. The comb and wattle of the bird would be removed for the fight in a process known as dubbing, not only to enhance the ferocious appearance of the bird, but also to limit wounding. Cock-fighting was banned in the UK in 1849, although care must be taken to keep mature cocks separate as they will fight to the death. The breed became popular as an ornamental fowl.

Enthusiasts began selective breeding to create a taller chicken with tighter feathering. Others disagreed with these changes and created the name 'Old English Game' for the earlier type. Two clubs were created: the Carlisle and the Oxford. Differences between the two were apparent; the Carlisle bred a bird with a horizontal back and a large breast in 13 varying colourways. The Oxford Old English Game was more alike to the original game fowl, being slender with a back at 45 degrees to the ground, with 30 colourways.

John Messenger

The main use for the Old English Game today is for exhibition, although they do lay 100–160 tinted eggs a year. They come in a bantam variety, and males are known to take over the incubation of chicks and even help rearing them – a behaviour unknown elsewhere in the chicken world. Mothers are extremely protective, producing slow maturing chicks who show fighting instincts from the start. This breed is not good for the beginner – the birds are noisy, aggressive and therefore not the right bird for mixed flocks. They are good foragers and need free range conditions. Mature cocks weigh 2.3kg; hens are 1.8kg. They have a long lifespan.

OLD ENGLISH PHEASANT FOWL

onby and Player

This chicken originates from England, in particular areas of Yorkshire and Lancashire. It was not given its name until 1914, when the breed society was formed, as a restoration of the Gold Spangled Yorkshire Pheasant Fowl and the Lancashire Mooney Fowls. It has similarities in appearance to a pheasant. These two breeds have been around for centuries but were thought to have been assimilated into the Hamburgh chicken with a focus on exhibition rather than utility points, until a search party began looking into isolated farms in the Yorkshire Dales and surrounding counties to find the original utility variety. The Old

English Pheasant Fowl has never interested commercial famers but they found a home with smallholders up to the 1950s.

The birds have a rose comb with a long leader, which trails the shape of the skull. They possess white, oval earlobes and have legs and feet which are slate-grey. There are two recognised colours: silver – which is very difficult to come by, and gold. The gold or silver feathers are tipped by a black half-moon.

The bird is known to be adaptable and multi-purpose. It lays 160–200 white eggs every year, depending on the strain, and the male has a very fleshy breast, especially for a light breed. The birds are natural foragers and need to be kept free range. They can withstand the cold and have a long-life span. For the majority of the time they are docile, although this is not to be tested at breeding time.

RHODEBAR

The Rhodebar was bred with the intention of creating an auto-sexing bird with the marketing properties of a Rhode Island Red. In contrast to most other auto-sexing breeds, which were contrived at Cambridge University, this bird was created at the University of British Columbia in Canada. The UK developed their first birds in 1947 from mixing a Danish strain of Rhode Island Red hens with Golden Brussbar cockerels. The resulting chickens were initially known as the Redbar. They were later termed Rhodebar, after a later type was developed in the early 1950s in a crossing programme comparable

to the creation of the Canadian Rhodebar. The British breed was standardised in 1952. As an auto-sexing breed it is possible to distinguish the pale male chicks from the barred (striped) female chicks at a day old.

Throughout the 1940s and 50s the Rhodebar was considered the most significant breed on the market, with the auto-sexing ability making it especially economical to produce. The bird is red with thin buff barring, comparable to the Rhode Island Red, but with a black tipped tail. Males weigh 3.6kg, females 2.7kg. 180–200 light brown eggs are produced each year. There is a bantam version, but these are very hard to find.

Mark Anderson-Howe

ROSECOMB BANTAM

The Rosecomb bantam is a true bantam, which means it is not derived from a larger chicken. Records of it go back to the fourteenth century in Britain, although the exact history is not clear. We do know that they caught King Richard III's eye in the fifteenth century and he kept an ornamental flock. They have enjoyed popularity over the years, finding their way to America and the first North American poultry exhibition, which was held in 1849 in Boston. By 1874 they had been entered into the American Standard of Perfection, which recognises three colours: black, blue and white, although there are 25 colourways in total.

RBST

They have been selectively bred for exhibition, which means that egg laying ability, meat and reproductive functions have been compromised. Chicks are difficult to raise, with high mortality rates. Hens produce 150–180 white/cream eggs every year. Cocks weigh 600g whilst hens are 500g. They are known for their striking, large rose comb, which needs to be looked after as cocks can suffer frostbite in cold weather. Having said that, these bantams can tolerate most climates and are friendly and easily handled, although cocks can be aggressive.

RUMPLESS GAME

This chicken, as its name suggests, is lacking tail feathers. The North American Araucana and Barbu d'Everberg chickens share this similar feature. They do not have a caudal appendage, which is otherwise known as the 'Parson's Nose' and they need this fleshy bone for the tail feathers to grow.

The bird comes from the Isle of Man, which is also home to the tail-less Manx cat. Rumpless Game bantams are also in existence. Edward Brown, who was a chicken expert in Victorian times noted that there were a prolific number of rumpless chickens on the Isle of Arran, which is not a million miles from the Isle of Man. So, it is presumed that the Rumpless Game was a cross between these Isle of Arran chickens and the Old English Game, which could be found in the vicinity. Their creation was surely helped by the invention of steamships, which opened up tourism in the mid-nineteenth century.

The breed is hard-feathered with an alert posture and forward-pushing deportment. The body is curved, with sturdy legs, a single comb, and small red wattles and earlobes. Colours can be red/black, black, wheaten, brown/red, cuckoo and grey or any such 'game' colour – indeed, all colours are recognised within the standard of the Poultry Club of Great Britain.

Cocks weigh 2.3–2.7kg, whilst hens are 1.8–2.3kg. They do not lay many eggs, which are small and brown. Very occasionally they will lay some blue, white or even green eggs. This is due to a recessive gene, which could be caused by historic infiltration by Araucana genes.

Best Rumpless Game Black/Red - Myles Simmons Junior

Nick Trott

They like to free range. The bantam is more popular that the fowl. They are an ornamental breed.

SCOTS DUMPY

The most defining feature of the Scots Dumpy is its short legs, which allow it to waddle. The legs are not more than 3.7cm long and support a large body, that can weigh in its entirety, up to 3.2kg. As suggested, the bird comes from Scotland, where it would have been a crofter's or cottager's fowl, providing meat and eggs, and clearing up any surplus food, preventing the occurrence of vermin. The fact that it could not travel very far, due to its short limbs, would be an added bonus to the crofter in its free ranging. Records of short-limbed chicken go back to Saxon times in 900AD. It is thought that the Picts and Celts used them during Roman invasions, as alarms whilst camping out during battle. Archaeological evidence in York shows the presence of short-limbed birds in the eleventh century, and they have been written about for centuries.

Scots Dumpies were first exhibited in London in 1852, but they lost out to the more exotic breeds, and numbers began to fall severely. A handful of steadfast breeders in Scotland saved the chicken during the 1970s, and it has since gained in numbers. It is known by many names, including 'Creepies', 'Bakies' and 'Stumpies'. The breed club was set up in 1993.

The characteristic of short legs is due to a dwarfing gene, comparable to the gene in Dexter cattle. This gene means that if two short-legged Dumpies are crossed, you will get 50 per cent offspring with

RBST

short legs, 25 per cent with longer legs and 25 per cent will either not develop at all or die once hatched. What breeders tend to do is mate a longer legged bird with a shorter one, creating 50 per cent long legs and 50 per cent short legs. The longer legged birds are good for the table. Colourways of black and cuckoo are most common, with blue and white also seen. There is a bantam version.

SCOTS GREY

The Scots Grey was once found extensively throughout the lowlands of Lanarkshire. It is known to have existed from the 1500s, living as a cottager's fowl and on farms, although its exact origins are hard to trace since it has gone by so many different names in the past, including: Chick Marley, Shepherd's Plaid, Greylings, Greylocks, Mauds and Chickmalins. Principle poultry chronologists believe that the Scots Grey evolved from the Scottish native fowl that would have been present on farms. The Scots Grey Club was formed in 1885 and the breed's popularity continued right up until 1940. The Scots Grey today is predominately bred for exhibition.

Historically, the Scots Grey would have been used as a dual-purpose bird, with males weighing 3.2kg and females 2.25kg. The hen rarely goes broody. Depending on the strain, she will lay 150–180 large, whitish eggs a year. There

is only one colour variation, that of barred. The base colour is steel-grey. The black barring has a metallic patina, similar to the Barred Plymouth Rock. There may be some black mottling on the legs. There is a bantam version.

The bird is hardy and can do well in most climates. Excessive sun will cause its feathers to go brassy. They prefer a free ranging lifestyle, and often choose to roost in trees.

SEBRIGHT BANTAM

The Sebright bantam was first devised by Sir John Saunders Sebright (1767–1846), who was the MP for Hertfordshire. He wanted to create an ornamental laced bantam, and documentation shows that he began with a Nankin, a Hamburgh and a Polish bird that exhibited lacing, to develop the gold laced Sebright. He then made the silver variety, by crossing some of the golds with white Rosecomb bantams that he purchased from London Zoo. The birds have uniform lacing in black on their plumage, with a foundation of either deep gold or bleached silver, with mulberry combs, earlobes and wattles, although today red is accepted. Sir John set up the very first poultry club for an individual breed. The Sebright bantam is a true bantam, meaning that there are no equivalents in the chicken world.

Sir John wrote extensively about his experiments and his work was read by Charles Darwin, particularly Sir John's pamphlet on *The Art of Improving the Breeds of Domestic Animals* (1809) which contained the passage: 'the weak and the unhealthy do not live to propagate their infirmities'. Indeed, Charles Darwin actually quoted from Sir John in his formative work *On the Origin of Species*, published in 1859, where he states 'That most skilful breeder, Sir John Sebright, used to say, with respect to pigeons, that "he would produce any given feather in three years, but it would take him six years to obtain head and beak"'. These are all wonderful insights in the work that was being done on selective breeding and natural selection in that time.

The Sebright bantam is very small. Cocks weigh 625g whilst hens are 570g. They have compact backs, big breasts and downward facing wings, giving them a perky, upright look. Hens lay 50–80 small, white eggs a year. There have been two centuries of inbreeding, creating limited fertility and high mortality rates amongst chicks. Cocks are unusual in that they are 'hen feathered'. They lack the long sickle-shaped feathering found in the tail, neck and saddle of most cocks, and share similar feathering to the hens. This has created interest amongst molecular biologists, who are keen to learn more about sex hormones.

SICILIAN BUTTERCUP

The Sicilian Buttercup traces its roots to the native chicken of the Italian island of Sicily. It can be seen in sixteenth century paintings in the Vatican, Rome, Florence and Paris and stands out because of its characteristic cup shaped comb. This is actually two combs, which are attached at the front and back, with the top edge jagged. This comb may be affected by frostbite.

It is believed that Sicilian immigrants bought the bird to the United States in the 1830s, but the first recorded importation to the US was by Captain Dawes in 1860. He commanded a ship

Jed Dw

called the *Frutiere*, and was on his way home to Dedham, Massachusetts with a cargo of oranges from Sicily. He purchased a collection of chickens that would supply meat for the voyage. He was impressed by the egg laying ability of these chickens, so he kept some for that purpose. When he got home, he sold a few to C. Carroll Loring who became the initial breeder in the line of Sicilian Buttercups. Success was achieved when Mr Dumaresq and Mr Audinger, owners of a poultry magazine, set up the American Buttercup Club 1908, achieving 600 members by 1914.

Two years before, in 1912, Mrs Colbeck of West Yorkshire had brought in some Buttercups from the States and a flourishing club was formed in the UK, with over 100 birds being entered for competition after the First World War. However, there was a massive reduction in numbers from the mid-1920s and the breed has struggled ever since.

There are two standardised colours, that of gold and silver. Roosters weigh around 3.0kg and hens 2.5kg. They are mainly bred for ornamental purposes. The hen will lay 50–80 small, white eggs a year. The birds like to free range and their testy, excitable temperament can be seen as a positive when the fox is prowling.

SPANISH

The presence of the Spanish chicken in the UK could date back to 1572 when records first note Spanish fowl. Imports of the Spanish breed have continued since then from both Spain and Holland. However, the chicken became British by the nature of its white facial features, which were expanded and improved by breeders in the UK, particularly in Bristol. The original Spanish birds only had white ear lobes. The breed is one the UK's more ancient chickens, broadly kept and enjoyed years before the poultry shows began in the late nineteenth century. The Spanish Club was also formed in the late nineteenth century. Subsequent DNA testing has shown the Spanish chicken to be one of the most unadulterated and defined of all breeds. Nowadays, there are fewer than 10 significant breeders. There is a bantam version, but they are very hard to find.

The Spanish, or White-Faced Black Spanish, had its hey-day in the mid-1800s, but by the start of the twentieth century it became very rare. Hens lay around 180 large white eggs per annum, taking a respite in autumn in order to moult. Birds have shiny black feathering with the defining large white face, which is especially striking on cocks. Judging standards give half the points for the head: 35/100 for the face and 15 for the comb and wattles. The face needs to be completely white with no red patches, or brown scabs. The hen's comb is folded, whilst the cocks is upright.

M.J. Winson

Akin to other Mediterranean chickens, the Spanish is energetic and agile, and a non-sitter. Females have a long life-expectancy, whereas males commonly die before they reach two years of age. This is due to poor weather conditions and the cold, which hampers the cocks as they lose a lot of heat through their combs and wattles. Culling of males should therefore never take place in the autumn. External runs must also be protected from the wind, rain and excessive sun. This breed is one for the expert and in order to achieve showing success, large numbers need to be maintained.

SULTAN

The Sultan chicken originally came from Turkey, where it was cultivated as a decorative breed for the Sultan of Constantinople (now Istanbul) to grace his gardens. They were brought to the UK in 1854 by Miss Elizabeth Watts, who lived in Hampstead Heath in London. She bred these birds and it is said that they are the ancestors of all the Sultans in the country, even though she only brought one hen over. Since that time, numbers have stayed small; however, a continuation of interested breeders have kept the Sultan alive, preventing too much inbreeding. The Sultan has always been bred for showing, and is not a good layer or table bird.

There is a bantam version but this is extremely rare. The breed standard only accepts white Sultan chickens. The head is the prominent feature, being both crested and bearded. They have profuse leg feathering and are one of the only breeds of chicken to have five toes. Their extensive white feathering can make them look meatier than they really are. This feathering is not so

Les Allan

apparent on a young chicken, but by the second year they attain their adult look. Both sexes have a white/light blue beak, red eyes and face, with vivid red ear-lobes, comb and wattles and white shanks and toes. The comb and wattle can sometimes get lost in the feathering.

The breed is friendly and docile, but hens do not have great maternal instincts. Chicks take a long time to mature. Due to their gentle nature, they can be harassed by more assertive breeds, preferring to be kept with birds of a more placid character. They are best kept in large runs, free from mud and other debris. They definitely need shelter in extreme weather, especially in the cold. Since they are good flyers, even a two metre high fence may not be enough to keep them contained!

SUSSEX

Sussex chickens were shown at the first poultry show, held at London Zoo in 1845. They were known as 'Old Sussex', 'Surrey Fowl' or 'Kent Fowl'.

However, they were not included in the initial poultry standard, the Standard of Excellence in Exhibition Poultry drawn up by William Bernhardt Tegetmeier, the English naturalist, in 1865. It was not until 1902 that they were officially recognised, with the colour ranges of light, red and speckled being described for the breed standard. The earliest of these was the speckled variety. The light was thought to be a result of breeding with Oriental breeds like the Brahma and Cochin, and possibly the Dorking, with its silver-grey plumage. The red variety initially had a black chest.

Other colours were soon to follow. The brown variety is said to have been shaped by the Indian Game. The buff did not evolve until the 1920s, closely followed by the white. The silver was formed in the 1930s by Captain Duckworth and the coronation was bred by Robert Whittington in celebration of the coronation of King Edward VIII in 1936 – an event that never happened due to his

RBST

abdication, with the crown instead going to his younger brother who was made King George VI.

The Sussex Poultry Club, formed in 1903, now recognises eight colour standards: the light, speckled, brown, silver, white, buff, red and coronation.

Before the beginning of the Second World War, after which commercial hybrid chickens became regular fodder, the Sussex and Rhode Island Red were the most popular meat breeds in Great Britain. Depending on the strain, hens produce 180–200 creamy/brown eggs per annum, some up to 250. They are an excellent choice for the beginner, as they are docile and friendly. They like to free range but can tolerate confinement. They come in a bantam version, which is more popular than the fowl. They are stocky birds, with a wide, flat back and a tail that should be kept at a 45 degree angle.

The light Sussex is a good choice for hybridisation and can be used with a 'gold' cockerel, for example, the Rhode Island Red, to create sex-linked chicks.

WELBAR

An idea came to Mr H. Humphreys of Eastwrey, Devon in 1940. He wanted to create an auto-sexing breed, as well as keeping the dark eggs produced by the Welsummer chicken. He got in touch with Professor Punnet, who had previously bred the Cream Legbar, for guidance. He then crossed the Welsummer with the Barred Plymouth Rock. Chicks hatched in 1941, and males were then bred again

with Welsummer stock. This produced the gold and silver Welbars, which were accepted by the Poultry Club of Great Britain in 1948.

As an auto-sexing breed, it is possible to differentiate the male chick from the female at one day old. The females have dark stripes, which the males lack; being yellow with a white headspot. Auto-sexing is useful for breeders as they can discard extra males. Other auto-sexing breeds include Legbars and Rhodebars.

The bird is active and upright. Wings are neatly tucked in and the expansive tail is held high. The cock makes a reasonable table bird, and the hen will lay 160–200 dark brown eggs per annum. There is a bantam version of this chicken.

Kate Arno

TURKEYS

A Priority Breed is represented by a *

Blue*
Bourbon Red*
British White*
Bronze*
Buff*
Cröllwitzer (Pied)*
Harvey Speckled*
Narragansett*
Nebraskan*
Norfolk Black*
Slate*

BLUE

The Blue turkey is difficult to define as it is an evolution of the Slate turkey but is all blue in colour and lacks the black speckling of the Slate. Blue turkeys breed true, but it is important to remember to cross-breed with a Slate every few generations as in time the blue colour dilutes. A Blue turkey can be bred from two Slate turkeys. The Blue turkey is black based, with two dominant slate genes, creating a continuous, ashy-blue colouring, with hens slightly lighter. The Slate is black based with only a single dominant slate gene. Black turkeys also result from this gene pool. They exhibit pink legs and feet which differentiates them from Norfolk Blacks and Spanish Blacks. Historically, the Slate turkeys were bred by farmers in the US so that they could identify their flock as they walked to market. Although the turkey tastes delicious, it never caught on commercially.

A very pale Blue turkey is called a Lavender. These can be afflicted with eye problems, with females suffering more than males. This can cause blindness and is thought to be genetic as it occurs all over the world. It is therefore considered risky to mate a Lavender with a Lavender, and it is better to bring in the Slate genes.

Poults are whitish grey with a tinge of blue. Mature males reach 11.3kg, whilst females can reach 8kg.

RBST

BOURBON RED

The Bourbon Red is named after Bourbon Country, in Kentucky's Bluegrass region, where it was developed in the late 1800s. Mr J.F. Barbee selectively bred turkeys of several different varieties – the Buff, Bronze and White Holland. The Buff originated in Pennsylvania, where darker red Tuscarora or Tuscawara Buffs were found. These birds were transported west by settlers heading for Ohio and Kentucky becoming the main foundation stock for the Bourbon Red.

Mr. Barbee created an attractive bird of a good size that was dark red with white wing and tail plumage. These were invariably breeding true. He named them 'Bourbon Butternuts' but this did not take off. It was only when he renamed them 'Bourbon Reds' that the public took interest.

The Bourbon Red turkey was accepted by the American Poultry Association in 1909. It was strenuously selected for meat production giving delicious meat, with the large breast desired. Breeders boasted that it would be bigger than the Mammoth Red, a forerunner to the Broad Breasted Bronze. It did gain massive popularity throughout the 1930s and 1940s and was a dominant market force, but when the broad breasted turkeys came along its popularity declined. Since the beginning of the twenty-first century there has been revived appeal

for the Bourbon Red, with its biological fitness, taste and durability, and it has found a niche market.

The bird has a rich, dark chestnut mahogany plumage with white flight and tail feathers. Tail feathers show a red bar across them near the tips. The beak is light horn at the tip with a darker base. The eyes are dark brown, and the legs start off with a reddish hue in the young, turning pink with age. Poults are beige, with brown markings. A mature adult male reaches 14.9kg, whilst a female will reach 8.1kg.

BRITISH WHITE

Fossils show that turkeys have been in existence for 10 million years. They are thought to have originated from Mexico, where white turkeys were recorded by the Aztecs. Evidence shows the presence of the white turkey throughout chronicled history, and the British White is thought to be a variation of other turkeys which contain a dominant white gene. Other white turkeys that have been farmed in the UK in years gone by include the Austrian White, the White Holland, and perhaps more marginally, the Beltsville Small. Nowadays it is hard to find a standard version of these birds as the commercially hybridised birds have become dominant.

RBST

Henry VIII was the first British monarch to eat turkey, but it was Edward VII who made it a traditional Christmas dish, supplanting the traditional peacocks which used to be eaten at the palace. Turkey was considered a luxury until the 1950s when it became economical for all.

Both hen and stag have a pure white plumage, with no off-white markings. The British White has dark blue eyes, with a white/horn coloured beak. The throat, wattles and legs are all pink, with the legs and feet being a fawn shade. The poults are pure white from birth. A stag will weigh in the region of 12.7kg, whilst a hen is 9kg. Around 10 million turkeys are consumed at Christmas in the UK, with the average weight being around 5.5kg.

Bronze

The Bronze turkey was developed in Europe, from whence it was shipped to America. It was bred there with the Eastern wild turkey which created a bigger, stronger bird than the European turkey, but with less of the wildness of the American turkey. The American Poultry Association accepted it into its Standard of Perfection in 1874.

By the end of the nineteenth and beginning of the twentieth century,

RBST

breeders started to selectively mate the Bronze to increase its size. These bigger birds were collectively named Broad Breasted Bronzes, whereas the original birds were termed Standard Bronzes. The Broad Breasted variety went on to be the most important meat bird in America, commanding the market for the following 20 years, up to the point where the Broad Breasted White exerted more power. Broad Breasted Bronzes cannot mate without the help of artificial insemination as they are so big. The Standard Bronze can reproduce without help, which along with other characteristics, puts it in the heritage classification. Collectively the Broad Breasted and Standard types are known as the Bronze turkey.

Both genders have a metallic bronze plumage, with occasional black and white markings, although not all birds breed completely true. This plumage is most akin to the wild turkey than any other breeds. The beak is a horn shade. Poults have black legs that become a horn colour when mature. A grown male can reach 18.1kg and a female 11.8kg.

BUFF

The Buff turkey, as you would expect, has rich cinnamon coloured feathers on its body. Their primary and secondary wing feathers are white with buff hues and their tail feathers are also white with a characteristic buff line at the tip. They originated in America and were accepted into the American Poultry Association as early as 1874. However, this popularity did not last. The Buff was used in the evolution of the Bourbon Red turkey, which in 1900 was successfully selectively bred for production. Buff numbers fell, with the American Standard of Perfection ceasing to recognise it from 1915.

However, in Britain, the Buff was having a heyday. The Buff Turkey Club was formed at the beginning of the 1900s, but although the bird was well loved, breeders had a lot of difficulty in selectively breeding the correct colourway. Nowadays, this trend continues with too many Buff turkeys showing Bourbon Red markings with black patches and white tails. Over time, commercial turkeys took the limelight and the Buff fell in popularity.

A new strain was created in the 1940s in the US, named the New Jersey Buff, after the place of its origin. However, this never caught on, as bigger turkeys, such as the Broad Breasted White, held the top spot in the market, refusing to let heritage breeds in.

Buff turkeys have a calm disposition making them easy to work with. They have not been selectively bred for commerce and are therefore smaller than supermarket turkeys. Males weigh 12.7kg and females are less, at 8.1kg,

taking five to six months to grow to full size. A lot of work is required to bring the Buff turkey back up to its standard colouration, however they would be ideal birds for a small-scale operation.

CRÖLLWITZER (PIED)

This turkey, otherwise known as the Pied or Black-laced White turkey has been in Europe from the 1700s. It is not a typical turkey, in that it has been selected for exhibition rather than meat production. It is a stunning bird to look at with the plumage of both male and females being black, white and black, and white, lending a pied appearance. Other similar turkeys can be found such as the Ronquire from Belgium and the American Royal Palm from the US. The Cröllwitzer is not large enough for the commercial meat market, but it is a superb choice for the smallholder as it is an excellent forager of

insects. Male birds weigh 10kg, females are 5.4kg. Eyes are pale brown and the beak light horn. The feet and legs are pink, reddening with maturity. At a day old, poults have a yellowish /white down. White feathers will grow through this and the distinct black colouration develops at 6–8 weeks.

HARVEY SPECKLED

This is a very recent addition to the Poultry Club of Great Britain. It was first admitted in March 2016 having been bred by Mr D.C. Harvey of Cornwall in the late twentieth century as a light commercial turkey.

The head is red, changeable to bluish white. The neck is creamy white with intermingling cinnamon speckles. The beak is light horn and the eyes have a dark hazel iris with a black pupil. The throat wattle is red, changeable to bluish white. Overall the plumage colour is creamy white, with distinct cinnamon speckles. The

RBST

flights and secondaries are creamy white, and the tail is also that colour. On the body, the under-colour and fluff is creamy white with some light cinnamon stippling. The legs and feet are salmon pink, with a touch of horn, ageing to horn. The female is less heavily speckled than the male. Day old chicks are creamy white with a darker mark on the back of the head. Defects would include a colour other than cinnamon, with speckles running into each other, and areas of solid colour, or barring of solid colour.

NARRANGANSETT

The Narrangansett turkey is named after its place of origin: Narrangansett Bay in Rhode Island. It is thought that English and European settlers bought the Norfolk Black to America, starting in the 1600s, and these birds were bred with the Eastern Wild turkey. A description in *The Poultry World* in 1872 describes flocks of 100–200 turkeys, bred from a handful of hens, feeding on grasshoppers, crickets and similar insects with hardly any additional feed. The American Poultry Association listed them in 1874. These birds became

RBST

the basis of the turkey food industry in New England, particularly in Rhode Island and Connecticut, but their influence also spread to the Mid-Atlantic States and the Midwest. However, by the early twentieth century the Bronze turkey had gained supremacy and the Narrangansett is only just making a comeback in niche markets, with consumers interested in biological fitness, ability to mate naturally and production methods.

The birds are known for their calmness and good maternal instincts, as well as egg production and early maturation of chicks. Narrangansett plumage is black, grey, tan and white. It looks rather like the Bronze turkey but lacks the coppery shades. White wing bars are a genetic mutation that are not found outside the US. It is hard to separate Narrangansett chicks from Bronze turkey chicks, as they are very similar until about six weeks of age. A mature male Narrangansett will weigh 14.9kg and a female will be around 10.4kg.

NEBRASKAN

Nebraskan turkeys were the result of a mutation that emerged in a closed flock of Broad Breasted Bronze turkeys back in 1947. The breeder, a R. H. Jandebeur of North Platte, Nebraska found that they bred true. There were three known colour varieties. One is the 'grizzled turkey' or Royal Nebraskan which had a mixture of grey and black feathering, with a broken pattern. Another colour variation is mainly white with black spots, and the third is the Spotted Nebraskan, which has a white base with spots of any colour except black, so there could be the Blue Spotted Nebraskan, the Red Spotted Nebraskan or the Buff Spotted Nebraskan. However, breeding pure strains within this colour frequency is difficult.

RBST

NORFOLK BLACK

This turkey originated from the Aztec birds of Mexico, where it was exported to Europe by Spanish adventurers in the early 1500s. Initially, the black colouration in turkeys was quite unusual in New World flocks. When the bird

arrived in Europe, it was selectively bred for this quality. It was also known as the Spanish Black and quickly spread throughout the Continent. In Britain, it was known as the Norfolk Black, and it is thought to be the earliest breed of turkey to have made a home in the country. It got its name from the popularity of the breed in East Anglia, and most especially in Norfolk, where the quality and flavour of its meat was highly prized. It takes around six months to raise a turkey for slaughter.

These black turkeys were shipped back to the Americas to be farmed by early colonists. There are suggestions that the first Thanksgiving feast, in 1621, was actually created using the Norfolk Black rather than the indigenous birds, with whom they shared a common ancestor.

The Norfolk Black has a long, deep body with notably wide shoulders. The plumage is a completely dark, matt black, with similar black legs, feet and toenails. The feet and legs become pink as the turkey grows older. An adult male weighs in the region of 11.35kg, whilst a female will reach 5.9–6.8kg. They have quiet temperaments and will lay from February to September, producing about 70 cream eggs with brown speckles per annum.

SLATE

The Slate turkey has unknown origins. Some say that it is bred from a cross between a Norfolk Black and a White Holland, although there is little genetic evidence to substantiate that. They were a true breed in the US in the late nineteenth century and were entered into the American Poultry Association's Standard of Perfection in 1874. In the UK they became very popular in the

1900s and were frequently exhibited in London at poultry shows.

They do have a delicious meat, which finds itself a home in niche markets. However, exhibition continues to be the dominant theme. Both sexes have a similar plumage but this can vary according to the genes. The Slate turkey exhibits the same colour variations as the Blue turkey, with turkeys showing as blue flecked with black spots, solid blue and solid black. A Blue turkey is black based, with two dominant slate genes, whereas a Slate turkey is black based with a single dominant slate gene, giving a slate feathering with black speckles all over the feathers. Without careful management, the flock will revert to the full colour spectrum, but the colour aimed for is an ashy blue with inconsistent black specks.

An adult male weighs 13.6kg, and a female is considerably smaller, at 5.4kg.

DUCKS

A Priority Breed is represented by a *

Abacot Ranger
Aylesbury
Black East Indian
Campbell
Cayuga
Crested
Magpie
Orpington*
Rouen (Exhibition)
Shetland*
Silver Appleyard
Silver Bantam*
Stanbridge White*
West Harlequin*

ABACOT RANGER

This light, dual-purpose duck was created between 1917 and 1922 by Mr Oscar Gray of Abacot Duck Ranch, Friday Wood, near Colchester in the UK. He found some white sports from his collection of Khaki Campbells and bred them with white Indian Runners. The resulting birds he called Hooded Rangers and put them to the test at the Wye College egg-laying trials in the period 1922–23, where they managed to lay an average of 233.75 eggs each for four ducks over the year and won first prize. Today's utility strains average 180–200 eggs yearly, which weigh 60–70g, similar to the Indian Runner.

After their conception, they were well liked utility birds, but fell from favour in the UK. If it was not for H. Lieker, who fortified the colour when the birds reached Germany by way of Denmark in 1926, the birds may well have become extinct. The breed was re-introduced to the UK in the 1970s and was regulated by the British Waterfowl Standard in 1983.

They are called the Streicherente in Germany and Eastern Europe, and Le Canard Steicher in France. They go by their original name in the US as Hooded Rangers, denoting the defined head colour. A group of breeders in the UK are working with German strains to regenerate the breed. Many UK bloodlines have been spoilt by crossing with Whalesbury hybrids (a mix between

Tim Daniels

the Aylesbury duck and the Welsh Harlequin), which create an incorrect bill and web colour. Abacot Ranger plumage colour changes from 'Nuptual' at breeding time to 'Eclipse', which is more concealing, the rest of the time. It is possible to determine the sex of the duckling by eight weeks – females have a dark grey bill, whereas males will have a sage-green bill. Drakes weigh 3kg and ducks 2.5kg.

AYLESBURY

The Aylesbury duck was raised in the town of Aylesbury in Buckinghamshire, and bred for its meat and feathers. It has a particularly large keel and is known for its white plumage and flesh coloured beak – although it has to be noted that not all white ducks are Aylesburys! Aylesbury was an historic centre for duck breeding going back to before the 1690s, and the white duck that preceded the Aylesbury was thought to be a white version of the wild Mallard, known as the White English. These ducks were selectively raised, and

RBST

by 1815 the Aylesbury took its name. It was prized for its feathers which were used extensively in quilts and bedding, and its light-coloured skin meant that it produced an agreeable looking carcass.

Ducks were bred in the fields outside Aylesbury and productive eggs were taken to 'Duck End', the area in the town where inhabitants would raise these ducklings inside their own cottages. Ducks were walked to market, making the long trek to London, covering 40 miles (64km) with their feet covered in tar, which would safeguard them from injury. Inns would supply pens, asking for a handful of birds in exchange for farmers resting at the end of the day.

This all stopped in 1839 with the opening of a railway line with links to London. By 1850, one ton of duck meat would be transported to Smithfield Market in London every day. Duck rearing became big business, and by the 1860s the heart of the operation moved out of Aylesbury town centre. Competition arrived in the form of the Pekin duck in 1873. It did not have the same succulence as the Aylesbury, but it was stronger and more economical to farm. Breeders began to change to Pekins or Pekin-Aylesbury mixes. By the end of the nineteenth century the Aylesbury breed was in decline. The two World Wars eliminated most farms and by the 1950s only one flock of Aylesbury ducks remained in the area. Duck farming in Aylesbury ceased in 1966.

The Aylesbury is a heavy breed: drakes weigh 4.5–5.4kg and ducks weigh 4.1–5.0kg. They lay few eggs, maybe 40–100 sizable eggs each year, determined by the strain.

BLACK EAST INDIAN

No one really knows where these stunning bantam ducks first came from. They were written about in the US at the beginning of the 1800s and were first recorded in Britain in 1850 or 1851 when they appear to have arrived from Buenos Aries with importations for the Earl of Derby. The name East Indian could have been given with inspiration from the East Indian Company, the British trading organisation, and this is entirely possible, as exotic and foreign birds were in demand, and the birds were priced accordingly. However, there is no evidence that the bird is linked to the Americas, north or south, although recently

Laura Ewan

gene scientists have hypothesised that it must have come from the northern hemisphere, possibly with Mallard ancestry, as it moults twice a year, whilst birds from the south shed feathers just once a year.

Whatever the ancestry, this little bird is a show-stopper. Its black plumage glistens with a beetle green sheen. It is not a great layer, producing 40–100 black eggs that fade to grey/white as the season progresses. They are energetic ducks and are light enough to fly, although their wings can be clipped until they feel at home. Females will often whiten with age, but this is due to extended black genes and cannot be bred out. Drakes weigh 900g and ducks are 700–800g.

CAMPBELL

The Campbell duck takes its name from Mrs Adele Campbell, who developed the bird in Uley, Gloucester in 1898, with the intention of creating a dual-purpose utility bird that matured quickly. She originally used a Rouen drake to mate with a Fawn and White Indian Runner, writing to The Poultry World in 1901 expressing that the Indian Runner had laid 195 eggs in 197 days. She went on to say, 'The original Campbells were practically this cross, except one season a Mallard drake was used.' The wild mallard was probably used to enhance the flavour of the meat.

At this time, buff coloured birds were the height of fashion, with William Cook releasing his Buff Orpingtons. Mrs Campbell tried hard to create a Buff Campbell and writing to The Poultry World in 1901 she says, 'and I thought of getting Buff too but failed. They would come out khaki. Just then the South African War was on, so I suppose it was patriotism.'

Graham Hicks

The khaki colour made Mrs Campbell think of British Army uniforms. The foundation of the Khaki Campbells was the original Campbell mated again to fawn and white Indian Runners.

Khaki is the most popular colour of the Campbell. It was released in 1901 but not standardised in Britain until 1926. The White Campbell was developed in 1924, by Captain F.S. Pardoe and was popular in that it gave a better-looking carcass. The Dark Campbell was developed some years later by Mr H. Humphreys in Devon, who was interested in producing a day old, sex-linked duckling using a Khaki drake. This variety was standardised in 1954.

Mrs Campbell's vision came off delightfully. The Campbell duck has been the most desired utility breed in the last century as the most prolific egg layer, producing up to 350 eggs per year, each weighing 2.5oz with a superb flavour. The Khaki Campbell is the most productive. Birds can lay from 5–7 months old. Drakes weigh 2.3–2.5kg and ducks are 2–2.3kg.

CAYUGA

This duck is named after Lake Cayuga to the west of New York, in the US. Its ancestry is not entirely clear. They are considered to have descended from the pure American Black wild duck (*Anas rubripes*) or been bought about by a

Adobe Stock

cross between that wild duck and the Mallard. They were initially recorded in the States between 1830 and 1850 and reached the American Standard in 1874. They were first shown in Britain at the Great Exhibition of 1851 at Crystal Palace and were standardised in the UK in 1901.

They are a heavy breed with the standard weight for a male at 3.6kg and 3.2kg for a female. They have a black bill, legs and feet, with corresponding plumage that shines an iridescent beetle green when it catches the light. The Cayuga lays 100–150 black eggs a year. This colour can be wiped off and the eggs become paler throughout the laying season. Ducklings are born black. Although the breed has undergone years of selective breeding to achieve its weight so that it now corresponds to the size of an Aylesbury or French Rouen, the black plumage creates black stubs in its breast when plucked, which consumers find unattractive. As a result, the white Pekin dominated the market in the US from 1873. There are better birds for meat and laying but the Cayuga is a good-looking bird and can fetch a high price.

CRESTED

The origin of these ducks is far from certain, but they were probably the descendants of the Bali Crested Runner duck which was transported to the Netherlands on trade ships from the Dutch East Indies. The Bali ducks resemble Indian Runners, with the addition of a small crest on their heads. In Holland they would have been developed further and crossed with regional ducks. Paintings going back 200 years represent crested ducks, and Dutch artists such as Melchior d'Hondecoeter and Jan Steen in the seventeenth century depict crested ducks in their work.

The crested gene can cause problems. If you mate two crested ducks together, 50 per cent of the offspring will be crested (although the crest may not always be in the right position). A further 25 per cent will be uncrested, whilst 25 per cent will die before hatching. It is therefore safer to mate a crested duck with a non-crested duck, where 50 per cent will be born with crests and 50 per cent without them. The crest position can be determined straight after hatching.

There is a bantam duck – the Crested Miniature, which was developed by John Hall and Roy Sutcliffe at the end of the last century. This was accepted by the British Standard in 1997. The Crested Duck was recognised by the

John Hall

American Standard in 1874, and by Britain in 1910. Any colour is permitted under the standard in Britain, as well as various other nations in the Continent.

Birds lay 120–200 eggs per year, and drakes weigh 3.2kg, whilst ducks are 2.7kg. They are not often shown, due to the challenges associated with the crest, and are more usually kept as decorative pets.

MAGPIE

In the 1920s there was a fashion for laying ducks, which was started in the 1900s by the Indian Runner ducks. The Magpie was developed by Rev. Gower Williams and Oliver Drake, although the ducks' parentage is not known. They do have a close resemblance to paintings of an earlier Belgium Huttegem breed, but share a comparable size and bulk with the Khaki Campbell. Although mostly white, the birds have a cap of black and black marking on the back. They also come in blue and white, chocolate and white, and dun and white. The latter two were developed in Germany. Since colour markings stay the same, it is possible to make an initial choice from the ducklings. One reason for the ducks' development was that black stubs would not be present on the breast when plucked, due to their light plumage in this area.

The birds lay around 220–290 large white eggs a year. Farmers with livestock have reported that since the ducks eat so many insects, slugs and snails, they

have helped to reduce liver fluke diseases. Although a lightweight duck, its meat is delicious, feeding 2–3 people per bird. Drakes weigh 2.7kg whilst ducks are 2.5kg.

ORPINGTON

The Orpington duck was developed in the late nineteenth century by William Cook with the intention of creating a dual-purpose utility breed. He was also responding to the fashion at the time for buff coloured poultry and he additionally created the Buff Orpington chicken during these years. Both breeds were named after his home town of Orpington in Kent and the duck was a combination of the Indian Runner crossed with Aylesbury ducks, Rouens and Cayugas.

The Buff Orpington duck was initially shown at the Dairy Show in Islington's Agricultural Hall, in London in October 1897 and was recognised by the British Poultry Standard in 1910. The Americans followed suit and the duck was admitted to the American Poultry Associations Standard of Perfection in 1914, known as the 'Buff Duck'. The Blue variety was accepted by the British Poultry Standard in 1926.

The duck also comes in Black, Chocolate and White, but these colours never attained a standard. Along with the Blue variety they appear to have gone

extinct. The Buff Orpington duck is an unstable colour as a result of a blue dilution gene. Offspring will result in three colours – buff (50 per cent), blond (25 per cent) and brown (25 per cent). It may be worth keeping the birds that do not reach the standard as they are good layers of up to 220 large white eggs a year, and although classified as a light duck they make good table birds, with drakes reaching 2.2–3.4kg and ducks 2.2–3.2kg. Eggs take 28 days to incubate. They are fun to keep as a hobby, and pet ducks tend to live for 8–12 years. They also have the added attraction of looking considerably cleaner than a white duck!

ROUEN (EXHIBTION)

Rouen ducks were originally developed in the eighteenth century around the French town of Rouen on the River Seine in Normandy. They stem from the wild Mallard, and similarities in plumage colour can be seen in both sexes. The Rouen was imported to the UK in the eighteenth century, where its size was further built up by discerning breeding. The artist Harrison Weir commented in 1902 that 'they are merely the wild duck enlarged by domestication and high feeding'. Weights of the exhibition strains can reach 5.5kg, with the birds sometimes crushing their own eggs due to their great bulk. They will lay 100–150 eggs a year, which are white with green/blue tints, and although valued for exhibition, they take eighteen months to reach their full weight and so are not considered a viable option for mass marketing, with white commercial ducks being preferred. They are known as the Giant Mallard. The production strain is smaller, 2.7–3.6kg, and lays more eggs.

Exhibition birds were standardised in the UK in 1865, being one of the first ducks to do so. They were established in North America by 1850 and recognised by the American Poultry Association in 1874. There is a blue variety but it does not breed true. They have been widely used as original stock for developing duck breeds in the twentieth century. They are too heavy to fly, and have a very calm, relaxed disposition and tame well.

Holtum and Benn

SHETLAND

The Shetland duck is a domestic duck that comes from the Shetland Isles in the northern most parts of Scotland. It is thought to have developed from the larger Pomeranian duck or Swedish Blue duck, with whom it shares many characteristics. The Vikings are charged with bringing this duck over to the UK. Up until the 1990s this species was believed to be extinct until a small number were discovered wild on the Shetlands and breeding programmes were put in place to enlarge the flock.

The birds are black, with their plumage flushed with green and blue like a Cayuga. They are small birds, only slightly bigger than a mallard. Unlike the Cayuga, they have irregular white breasts and occasionally white spots on their heads. As they age, the Shetland ducks' white feathering increases, sometimes turning totally white. The drakes have a yellowish bill and orange legs, whilst the ducks, which are slightly smaller, show black legs and bills. Males weigh in the region of 2kg, whilst females are 1.8kg. Due to their small size they are not suitable for meat. Ducklings are black or dark brown with yellow flecks.

They are quite tough little birds, always foraging, and are valuable for smallholders and novices as they are simple to keep. They are more productive

than the Campbells and Welsh Harlequins (a breed descended from the Campbells) as they even lay through to January in mild regions, laying 30–50 sizable white-grey eggs per year, each weighing around 50g.

SILVER APPLEYARD

The Silver Appleyard duck was developed in the 1930s by Reginald Appleyard, an expert poultry breeder and writer, at Priory Waterfowl Farm near Ixworth, Suffolk. He intended to create the 'Ideal Duck', which would provide both meat and eggs, but also be used for exhibition. A few years later he was winning prizes for these birds at the Dairy Show in London and Bethnal

John Green

Green. Ernest George Wippell painted a pair of these ducks in 1947. Whilst Appleyard continued to evolve the breed, when he died in 1964, a standard still had not been recognised. When the standard was eventually produced in 1982, it drew much inspiration from Wippell's painting.

Appleyard created a heavy breed, (drakes weigh 3.6–4.1kg, ducks weigh 3.2–3.6kg), that could reach a 3kg plucked weight by nine weeks old with a superb meat to bone ratio, whilst also able to lay a substantial quantity of large, white eggs (200–270 per year). It is known to be one of the best utility breeds of duck.

Interest in poultry declined after the Second World War and the Silver Appleyard became endangered. Tom Bartlett of Folly Farm, Gloucestershire maintained 130 different poultry breeds for public show and he was key in saving the Appleyard in the late 1980s, even creating a miniature version, which is not quite small enough to be called a bantam.

Silver Bantam

This duck was developed in Suffolk shortly after the Second World War in the 1940s, when Reginald Appleyard wanted to create a bantam version of his Silver Appleyard duck, as bantam chickens were becoming popular, and he could see the possibilities for a bantam duck. He bred a White Call drake with a smaller Khaki Campbell duck. The resulting birds were called Miniature Appleyard, but they looked more like the Abacot Ranger than the Silver Appleyard duck.

Later down the line, in the 1980s, Tom Bartlett of Folly Farm, Gloucester devised a novel bantam variety of the Silver Appleyard, using the bigger duck as a starting point. The bantam duck had the same colouration as the larger version. He called this new bantam duck the Silver Appleyard Miniature. After great consideration, Reginald Appleyard's version was renamed from the Silver Appleyard Bantam to the Silver Bantam.

The Silver Bantam was standardised in the UK in 1982, first as the Silver Appleyard Bantam and later in 1997 as the Silver Bantam, at the same time that the Silver Appleyard Miniature was recognised by the PCGB. The Silver Appleyard Miniature has gained in popularity at the expense of the Silver Bantam.

Ducks weighs 800g, drakes are 900g. You can expect 60–160 eggs per year.

RBST

STANBRIDGE WHITE

This medium sized duck originated in Romsey, Hampshire in the early twentieth century when Lord Greenway noticed that some of his Magpie ducks had laid pure white chicks. These he developed into the Stanbridge Duck, which were accepted by the Poultry Club of Great Britain in the 1920s. They all but went extinct, until in 2007 the President of the RBST found some in Gloucestershire, in the care of William Osbourne, who had bought them from an elderly chap living in Aylburton, Gloucestershire. All attested bloodlines go back to William Osbourne's ducks, when in 2009, he owned 14 Stanbridge ducks and four drakes. However, this is thought to number no more than two bloodlines. William said that the ducks 'start to lay in the first week of February and go on until at least October averaging about 240–250 eggs per duck' annually. The Poultry World Magazine in 11 April 1930 stated that they are 'a duck with proven merits which can challenge other more well-known egg laying breeds in terms of egg numbers, extended laying season and are also a good table bird'.

They resemble their founder breed, the Magpies – a breed from Wales, developed at the same time, although they are usually heavier. They have an alert carriage and deep, wide, pure-white body with a yellow/orange bill and orange legs. Eggs are slightly green at the beginning of the season. Drakes weigh 2.5–3.2kg, whilst ducks are 2–2.7kg.

WELSH HARLEQUIN

This lightweight duck was developed in 1949, in Hertfordshire, by Group Captain Leslie Bonnet, a keen breeder of utility ducks. His Khaki Campbell ducks produced two pale coloured offspring which he mated together, calling them Honey Campbells. In 1950 he moved with his family to live in a farm in Criccieth, North Wales and renamed the ducks, Welsh Harlequins. Bonnet records in his book *Practical Duck Keeping*, published in the 1960s, that his flock of ducks would lay 300 eggs each, per annum. These eggs are large and white,

and weigh in the region of 75–85g each. They are remarkable layers and in real terms, average 240–330 eggs per year.

The breed was first imported to Tennessee in the US in 1968 by John Fugate, as hatching eggs. Live ducks were taken to the US in 1981. Welsh Harlequins were recognised by the British Standard in 1997, with the US taking until 2001 to admit them to the American Poultry Association Standard of Perfection. They are now considered critically endangered in both countries.

Distressingly, the majority of Bonnet's flock was killed by a fox in 1968, but luckily Eddie Grayson retained a few of the earliest Welsh Harlequins and bred them with an original line of Khaki Campbells, thereby rescuing the breed.

The birds are dual purpose, providing a lean carcass, of 2.3–2.7kg, which is suitable for marketing. The birds have a colourful plumage and are much calmer than their founder, the Khaki Campbells. They don't fly much, making them suitable for the garden or backyard. They are keen foragers. Although initially very popular, their numbers dropped in the 1950s and 60s as did so many other duck breeds. Ducklings can be sexed easily a few days after hatching, with 90 per cent accuracy. The females have a lighter bill than their brothers, with a dark spot on it. After several days, this differentiation vanishes.

GEESE

A Priority Breed is represented by a *

Brecon Buff*
Buff and Grey Back*
Embden (As standardised in the UK) *
Pilgrim*
Roman*
Sebastopol*
Shetland*
Toulouse (Exhibition)*
West of England*

BRECON BUFF

The Brecon Buff was selectively bred by Rhys Llewellyn in 1929 in Wales. He was travelling through the Brecon Beacons, when he came upon a flock of grey and white geese. In the midst of these birds were some buff specimens. He immediately procured them and set about mating them with an Embden gander. The goslings were all grey, but he carried on, and in 1930, mated another two buff females. This time he got the result that he wanted: he had several buff offspring. He continued his experimentation and by 1933 his new breed, the Brecon goose, was breeding 70 per cent true to type. A year later, in a total of just 4–5 generations, he

Colin Murt

reached his goal of 100 per cent. That same year, in 1934, the Poultry Club met on 12 October and accepted the breed as standard. These findings were published in *The Feathered World* on 19 October.

The Brecon Buff must have pink bills, legs and webbing on their feet in order to be accepted as standard. Orange bills, although being the more dominant colour, are not accepted. The gosling will develop a pink bill as they fledge. White feathers under the chin are not allowed, although white feathering is allowed around the bill as this is a natural sign of aging. The buff feathering is edged by a paler colour, sometimes almost appearing white. They have deep brown eyes. The Brecon Buff is a medium sized goose, with the gander weighing 7.3–9.1kg and the goose 6.4–8.2kg. They are kept for their meat and eggs, and will lay 10–20 white eggs a year, with an incubation period of 28–34 days. There are not many geese that originate from the UK and they are easily distinguishable from the American Buff by their smaller size and their characteristic pink bills and feet. They are hardy by nature and good grazers.

BUFF AND GREY BACK

Pyde geese were mentioned in literature by Gervasse Markham in 1615 in the UK. This is before the introduction of the Toulouse, proving that neither the

Embden or Toulouse were the ancestors of the Buff and Grey Back, although the Buff and Grey Back do share the same shape as the English Embden.

These pied geese are typical of utility geese that have been bred for centuries in parts of Europe bordering the North and Baltic Seas, although different geese are of varying size and shape. They are usually known

Colin Murton

as 'Saddlebacks', referring to the white background with buff or grey spots on the head, neck, saddlebacks and thigh coverts. There are many similarities to the Pomeranian geese, but the Buff and Grey Backs have dual lobes and an orange beak and feet. The Buff and Greys also have blue eyes and are long-bodied. The breed was standardised in the UK in 1982.

They are a medium sized bird, with a gander weighing 7.3–10kg, whereas a goose is 7.3–9.1kg. She will lay 25–35 white eggs in spring. If kept as a pair, or trio, the goose will become broody.

EMBDEN

This breed is thought to have originated in the town of Emden in Lower Saxony, Germany, according to the writer Lewis Wright in 1900. Other thoughts are that it developed in the North Sea regions of the Netherlands and Germany, although Edward Brown wrote in his book *Races of Domestic Poultry* in 1909, that he thought the breed was descended from a cross between a German White and an English White. Other ideas include the emergence of the Embden by selective breeding with Toulouse geese or, even going back to the thirteenth century, descending from the Great White Landrace of Frisia.

Whatever its origins, the Embden is an impressive bird. It is the largest of all geese, standing a metre high and weighing 12.7–15.4kg for a gander, with females reaching 12.7kg. Quite often, in shows, the gander is judged according to its dead weight. UK Embdens are shorter and stockier than their European cousins, but heavier than those found in the US. They are completely white, with a short, light orange bill with a flesh coloured bean, and matching orange feet, which are relatively short. They have clear blue eyes in an oval head, with a long arching neck, long back and small tail. The wings are long and

Colin Murton

very powerful and are used in defence, especially during nesting time when the gander will hiss and ruffle his feathers to protect his young. They are not a beginner's breed and can be dangerous around small dogs.

Like other geese, the Embden is an omnivore and likes to forage in grass and water, eating small fish, snails and anything else they can find. If enclosed, they will strip an area bare, even destroying trees by eating the bark. The Emden is known as the Bremen in the US and L'oie d'Emden in France. In Germany they call the bird Emder Gans. The Embden goose was accepted by the British Poultry Standard in 1865 and the American Standard of Perfection in 1874.

Embden hybrids are one of the most frequently used geese in commercial production across Europe, but it is not to be confused with its hybrids. The Embden will be quite a lot larger than the hybrids and its blue eyes are a giveaway. It is often mated with the Toulouse or other large geese. The Embden is a good goose for the table and produces around 30 eggs in spring with an incubation period of 28–34 days. Goslings can show grey feathers on their back or rump for the first year of their life.

PILGRIM

The Pilgrim goose has uncertain origins. What has been documented is the journey, or pilgrimage, made by Oscar Grow, an expert on waterfowl, from Iowa to Missouri, during the Great Depression in the 1930s. His wife named the geese that they took with them after this epic journey of over 300 miles. The breed became widely known as the Pilgrim in the US from 1935 and entered into the American Poultry Association's Standard of Perfection in 1939.

But the mystery remains as to how the Pilgrim goose got there. Many believe that it went over to the US with early colonists, with the goose stemming from Western England and Normandy in France. There are several early accounts of geese matching the description of the Pilgrim in farmyards across Britain. They refer to white ganders and grey geese with an auto-sexing ability in the chicks. The Embden, introduced to Britain in 1815, as well as the Toulouse, subsequently became extremely popular, leaving the Pilgrim to hang on in small pockets in the south west. The Pilgrim was not included in the Poultry Club Standard until 1999.

Ganders are mostly white, maybe having some light grey plumage on the back, tail and wings. The females are totally different and are a pale grey (softer than that of the Pomeranian or Toulouse). The female's face may also be a soft grey, but this can turn white with age. Both sexes have orange legs and bills as adults, with the male having blue eyes and the female brown.

The Pilgrim is an auto-sexing bird, which is

Colin Murton

when pure bred chicks can be told apart according to their gender, from even a day old. The males will be silver-yellow with a pale orange bill, and the females olive-grey with a darker bill. Feather colour may take 12–14 days to ascertain, but bill colour is obvious from day one – the females will have the darker bill. The only other auto-sexing goose in Britain is the West of England goose, and the female of that species has blue eyes.

Pilgrim geese have a wonderfully docile nature, especially if they have been well handled when young. Males are noticeably endearing and watchful of their females. A Pilgrim goose can live for 15 to 25 years. Weight can be from 6.4–8.2kg for the gander and 5.4–7.3kg for the goose. The females will often lay two clutches, a total of about 30 eggs, between February and June.

ROMAN

The British Roman goose is said to have its roots in ancient Rome, 2,000 years ago, where it was thought to be sacred to Juno, the goddess of marriage. In 365BC the Gauls made an attack on Rome in the dark of night, and it was the honking of this very goose which saved the city from destruction. Small, white geese are popular all over central Europe, with the Diepholtz goose being slightly bigger and the Czech goose a little smaller.

The Roman goose was bought to the UK from Italy, Germany and Poland in the early 1900s. They were accepted into the British Poultry Standard in 1954. In the UK, both tufted and non-tufted varieties are accepted, whereas in the US, the American Standard of Perfection, entered in 1977, identifies them as ornamental and prescribes a tuft.

The geese are white with light blue eyes and an orange/pink bill, webs and feet. Occasionally they will show grey or buff feathers. Goslings may have some grey feathers, but this will be molted out within a year. Whilst it is an exhibition bird in the US, in Europe it is kept for meat. Although small, the Roman goose provides a plump bird for the oven, weighing 5.4–6.4kg for the male and 4.5–5.4kg for the female. A female will lay up to 60 eggs per year and the birds will live for 25 years if not taken by the fox. Similar to other geese, they are well mannered if handled well as a gosling. Ganders can be bred with 2–4 geese.

SEBASTOPOL

Sir Edward Brown, writing in 1929, alleged that Sebastopols were imported to the UK in 1859, after the end of the Crimean War. They arrived in Ireland in 1863 and were known as Danubian geese, being prevalent in all the countries adjacent to the drainage basin of the River Danube, which runs into the Black Sea. In France they are known as L'oie Frisse and in Germany, Lockengans or Struppgans, translating as 'curl-goose' or 'unkempt goose'. They were shown at the Crystal Palace Poultry Show in 1860 and entered the British Poultry Standard in 1982.

Sebastopols are sometimes called the 'pantomime goose' for their unique appearance. They come in two different categories; the smooth-breasted and the curl-feathered, both of which are standardised in the UK, as well as the two colourations, Buff and White. The smooth breasted has an extremely elongated feathering from the scapular and thigh, with a thick sward of fine tresses frequently touching the ground. The curl-feathered type shows a profusion of strong ringleted feathers in the body, with the wings and thighs exhibiting strands and tendrils. Their legs and shanks are orange and they

have vivid blue eyes. Birds weigh in the region of 5.4–7.3kg for males, and 4.5–6.4kg for females. Breeding in the UK over the last centenary has increased body weight by around 30 per cent. The feathering on these birds prevents them from flying.

The goslings are auto-sexing, which is generally thought to be reliable, with the females darker than the males. They are a medium weight goose and not considered to be aggressive. They are kept for their meat, or ornamentation. In the past, their feathers would have been utilised for bedding, pillows and quilts. They will produce up to 40 eggs per year. They require a shed in which to shelter from rain, as their back feathers are not so resilient as other geese. Sebastopols need access to plenty of clean water to keep their feathering clean.

SHETLAND

The Shetland goose, as its name suggests, come from the Shetland Islands to the north of Scotland, where they have been documented from the seventeenth century. In these islands, which are 60 degrees North, the birds must be tough to cope with the powerful winds and a winter with no more than six hours of daylight per day. Similar to other Shetland breeds, the goose is small, weighing between 5.4–6.4kg, and is about 2/3 the size of a standard goose. As you would expect, they are excellent foragers, able to find grit and grass even under heavy snow. Their bills are adapted for this by being slightly shorter, and crofters would put a flock of geese out to pasture before their sheep, as the geese would cleanse the field of parasites without themselves coming to harm, in particular clearing out liver fluke, which can be potentially fatal to sheep.

These geese are extremely rare. They were initially exported to a farm in New York State, in the US in 1997, although they have not yet been admitted to the Standard of Perfection. It is feared that the gene pool in North America is not big enough to create viable populations, and the geese suffer from crooked toes, kinked necks, wry tails and diminished vigour through lack of genetic diversity. They are, as a result, under the watch of the American Livestock Breeds Conservancy.

The geese do mate for life, which is why it is futile to have more than one goose per gander. They make excellent parents and can live more than 20 years. The parents are sexually dimorphic and the chicks can be auto-sexed. Male chicks are white and females grey. In the adults, the gander's feathers will be totally white, whilst the goose will have a grey head, neck and upper body with only a white underbelly. He will have blue eyes, whilst she will have brown, which may be specked with blue. They both have pink legs. She will lay about 30 white eggs a year.

TOULOUSE (EXHIBITION)

The Toulouse, as its name suggests, originated near Toulouse, in southern France. The birds are known as L'oie du Toulouse in France, and Toulouser Ganz in Germany, and are descended from the European Greylag Goose, *Anser anser*, the common ancestor of geese in the West. They were bred for culinary use in the French dish, Pâté de foie gras, which is comprised of deliberately fattened goose or duck liver. The process of achieving this is controversial as the birds are often force fed, with tubes pushed down their throats and fat and grain mash being passed through them, resulting in an enlarged, often diseased, liver.

Prior to the 1950s, a lot of birds were exported to Canada and the US. Some of this gene pool is now returning to the UK to increase diversity, as males in the UK are tending to become infertile.

Birds are classified as Production, Standard Dewlap or Exhibition. The Exhibition birds are the biggest, with ganders reaching 11.8–13.6kg and geese 9.1–10.9kg. They have pronounced dewlaps, which are folds of skin that fall

Colin Murton

from the base of their bill to the top of their neck. Exhibition birds are bred for the show ring. They are so huge that their body often touches the ground. The Standard Dewlap Toulouse Geese is bred for food production, including the foie gras of above. They are very difficult to breed, but gain weight rapidly, reaching 9.1–13.6kg+. The Production Toulouse goose is smaller at 8.2–9.1kg and is the kind found on farms, where they are kept for meat and eggs, of which they lay 25–40 per year.

The colouration is predominantly grey: pearly grey being more popular than dark or brown grey. They have been bred in white, which was standardised in the UK in 1982, and in buff, standardised in the UK in 1997. The grey variety has been standardised in Britain since 1865.

The birds can live to 20 to 22 years, but as many of them are overweight they tend to live only 10 years. They mate for life, although it is suggested that one gander can be put to three to four geese. They need protection from prolonged rain, as their softer feathers lose their oil more quickly than other geese. These geese require a pond to bath in, after which they can preen and re-oil their feathering. The Toulouse are perfect farmyard pets as they are incredibly docile, although they can be difficult to breed. The goose can crush her eggs with her sheer weight, although a big tray, lined with hay can help her find her ground. Occasionally a Muscovy goose will foster the white eggs.

After 28–34 days, the goslings will emerge. They will have greenish-grey down, with black legs, feet and bill. As adults they will not be able to fly, due to their great size, and will have an orange bill, brown eyes and reddish-orange legs and feet. Their eyes will be lined with orange. They will have a long, broad body with an exceptionally deep breast. Their heads will be big with a huge dewlap, overlapping in ripples down their throat to their neck. They are susceptible to flystrike, which is an attack of maggots on open wounds. This can be hard to see due to their ample feathering.

WEST OF ENGLAND

The West of England goose is thought to pre-date 1600 and has existed in farmyards throughout the UK, particularly in the West Country from at least that time. It was first standardised in the UK in 1999. It is known for its similarities to the Pilgrim goose, not just in its size and colouring but also for its auto-sexing ability. Some think that its ancestors were taken to the US with the colonists, which is a distinct possibility, where successive breeding created the Pilgrim that we know today.

The auto-sexing ability is of great appeal to goose breeders as geese are notoriously problematic to sex. These geese can be sexed at pipping, as the young bird cracks open the egg. The males have a pale orange beak, whilst females have grey patches on their beak. As adults the sexual dimorphism continues, with the gander being white with the odd grey patch, and the female with a grey neck and head, and a pied saddleback. Both have a pale pink/orange bill, legs and webbing.

Countless generations of breeding on farms may have resulted in inbreeding with reduced stature. The males tend to weigh between 8.6–10.0kg and females are 7.7kg. She will lay 20–50 big, white eggs every year and he will become extremely defensive when she is sitting on her eggs, like other geese. However, the breed is an exceptionally placid one and ideal for the beginner. The breeding season is between the end of February to the end of April and is perfect for anyone with a bit of land who wants meat, eggs, mowing and a burglar alarm all wrapped up in one.

RBST